Hexham Abbey ₨

The Hexham Abbey Project
2009-2017

Edited by
Chris Tolan-Smith and Peter Richmond

HEXHAM LOCAL HISTORY SOCIETY
2017

Hexham Local History Society
Hexham, Northumberland

www.hexhamhistorian.org

First published 2017

ISBN: 978-0-9527615-9-4

Cover Design by Peter Rodger based upon a watercolour portraying Hexham Abbey before 1860, though created several decades later by Paul Braddon (1864-1938). Hexham Abbey collection HEXAB3003

Printed by Lightning Source UK, Milton Keynes, MK11 3LW

Contents

Figures

Figures

Preface

The need for improved facilities at Hexham Abbey had been acknowledged for most of the 20th century but it was not until 2009 that a plan was finally embarked upon that led to the major project that is celebrated in this volume. The decision by the Ministry of Justice to close the Magistrates' Court on 1st April 2011 was unpopular, but it did provide an opportunity for a much greater part of the former priory to be reunited with the Abbey church after an interval of nearly 500 years. For most of the past decade work has been undertaken to both expand our understanding of the Abbey and its treasures and to enhance the fulfilment of its mission. Much of what has been achieved is summarized in the following chapters.

We begin with a summary of the gestation and implementation of the project (Chapter 1). This is followed by a review of previous schemes that came to nothing (Chapter 2) and an account of the recent refurbishment of the priory buildings (Chapter 3). This work had to be preceded by a careful study of the archaeology and history of the buildings in question (Chapter 4). In addition to studying the buildings and developing their facilities, an important aspect of the project has been to pay attention to the Abbey's many treasures including architectural stone work (Chapter 5), liturgical fittings (Chapter 6), historic prayer books (Chapter 7), and church vestments (Chapter 8).

Lastly, a team from the Centre for the Study of Christianity & Culture at the University of York has shown how an innovative use of digital mapping technology can be deployed as both a research tool and a way of enhancing our experience of a major historic site (Chapter 9).

The work at Hexham Abbey from 2009 to 2017, described in this book, should be seen as the initial phase of a continuing programme of research and enhancement.

The editors would like to express their sincere thanks to Professor Richard Bailey who kindly read an early draft of the book and made many helpful suggestions. Remaining errors are the responsibility of the authors. We are also grateful to the Hexham Local History Society for their assistance as publishers of this volume and to their Chair, Peter Rodger, for designing the cover.

List of contributors

Chris Britton, Hexham Abbey Conservation Team

Christopher Cotton, RIBA, AABC, of Purcell UK, Hexham Abbey Architect

Hugh Dixon, MBE, MA, Dip. Hist. Art (Edin.), FSA, Hexham Abbey Conservation Team

Louise Hampson, MA, Centre for the Study of Christianity and Culture, University of York

Thomas Kelsey, B.Sc., Ph.D., Hexham Abbey Conservation Team

Neel Lever, Hexham Abbey Conservation Team

Peter F Ryder, BA, M.Phil., FSA, Independent Archaeologist

Christine V Seal, BA, M.Phil., Ph.D., Hexham Abbey Conservation Team

Revd Canon Chris Simmons, MA, Retired Priest, Hexham Abbey

Christopher Tolan-Smith, BA, Ph.D., Hexham Abbey Conservation Team

[Contact details can be provided on request: Hexham Abbey Conservation Team, Parish Centre, Hexham Abbey, NE46 3NB]

[*Editorial note:* Items in the Abbey collection are identified in the relevant footnotes by their HEXAB catalogue numbers. An extract from the catalogue is available online via the Heritage page on the Abbey website: www.hexham-abbey.org.uk]

Acknowledgements

The plans in Figure 14 are used with the kind permission of Chris Cotton, Purcell UK. All images in chapter 9 (Figures 59 to 64) are ©The Centre for the Study of Christianity and Culture, University of York, and are reproduced with permission. Most other figures are photos of items in the Abbey's collection, or drawings, by the respective authors. Exceptions: Figures 1 to 3, 5, 16, 34 to 38, and 40 to 46 are by Chris Britton; Figure 4 is by Tony Iley; Figure 18 is by Chris Tolan-Smith; Figures 57 and 58 are by Tom Kelsey.

Foreword

Back in 1898 the then Rector of Hexham, Canon Sydney Savage, wrote to *The Times* newspaper with a vision for a museum at Hexham Abbey. Despite numerous ideas and plans over the subsequent decades, nothing materialized.

This book explores some of the story around how that changed: it took the right buildings to be available; it took the dedication and energy of a whole team of people; it took the generosity of funders — both the Heritage Lottery Fund and major trusts, but equally importantly those local people who came up with a huge number of inventive ideas.

Above all it took prayer and conversation to discern what God might be calling us to do as a community. Knowing that we had an incredibly special set of buildings and a wide constituency of people who had an opinion about them, the project took time to coalesce as different elements came together. Sometimes this was frustrating, even despairing, but we knew that we were building on ancient foundations and creating something that would, hopefully, serve God's loving purposes for the people of Hexham and Tynedale over the next few centuries.

Our vision was formed around revealing the past, enhancing the present, and enriching the future.

Much was discovered about the Abbey's past and the story of the former monastic buildings began to be unpicked as work progressed and light shone into previously blocked-up doorways.

We were keen to enhance the welcome that the Abbey provides to visitors and pilgrims, as well as our ability to host groups, mark events along life's journey, and foster a stronger community.

This was all set within a hope that more people would encounter God in Jesus through how the Abbey, in silence and song, speaks to them, via the host of activities that go on across the site, and in the love, compassion, and joy which should always be at the heart of the congregation's life of worship and service.

Time will tell how all of this settles into the rhythm and pattern of the Abbey's days. My prayer is that the Abbey will continue to be a place where God's love is enjoyed, celebrated, and shared.

✠ Graham Dudley

The Rt Revd Graham Usher, Bishop of Dudley
(Rector and Lecturer of Hexham, 2004-2014)

Hexham Abbey Revealed

1. Conservation Aspects of the Abbey Project

Tom Kelsey

Introduction

For many years prior to 2007, various proposals had been examined by Hexham Abbey for the provision of meeting and function rooms and associated facilities either as new build or using part of the existing medieval structures.[1] When the possibility of occupying former Northumberland County Council offices arose in 2008, further plans were developed and with parish and Heritage Lottery Fund (HLF) backing and a major fundraising effort, the Project delivery phase began. An associated business plan which had to be approved by HLF envisaged various sources of income to cover running costs, with HLF support in the first few years.

The formal aim was to develop the former Priory buildings as an iconic welcoming environment to draw in people from within and outside the Abbey community to participate, to learn, and to be inspired.

However, after approval of the 2009 plans, a further part of the monastic buildings unexpectedly became available with the closure in 2011 of the Hexham Magistrates Court and associated offices. A decision was made to adjust the plans and to purchase and include these new facilities.

The detailed project plans thus involved restoring the major part of the former monastic buildings for Abbey use, to create an educational facility, a high quality permanent exhibition for all ages, the launching of a welcoming café, the provision of quality function areas, and the institution of a conservation plan.

Originally developed by the then Abbey consultant architect, Mr Nick Rank, a formal Conservation Plan was submitted to the Heritage Lottery Fund covering cataloguing, conservation of the Abbey heritage, and involvement of the public outside the Abbey. A Conservation Advisory Panel was established to review and develop progress and a gradually-increasing team of volunteers started to implement the plan.

Some further aspects of the conservation work are detailed below, particularly in cataloguing and contributions from members of the public.

---

[1] See Chapter 2, p.11 et seq.

Cataloguing

One of the major benefits of pursuing the cataloguing process has turned out to be appreciation of the treasures that the Abbey holds — not just in number but in quality. Associated with this process was the creation of photographic records, for example of the roof bosses [Fig.1][2] and windows, to a higher quality that had been achieved in the past.

Fig.1: Early roof boss in the south transept

Enquiries around the museum industry as a whole led to a choice of the commercial Calm software as a record base which also happened to be used by the Northumberland Archives at Woodhorn and by York Minster for their archives and collections. It has proved a versatile choice, albeit needing some expert management. The Calm catalogue currently has records for well over 2500 items ranging from books to stained-glass windows. It assists in

---

[2] HEXAB362.7.

assembling the overall heritage and care needs of items, but is, importantly, the vehicle for accepting additional information about the objects listed. For example, an enquiry on the Abbey website about a painting or a window will probably have the answers available, under the HEXAB[3] catalogue reference number, together with any references to associated items. The records also provide a better level of security since every item is photographed with its details. However, like all software packages, one has to adapt day-to-day procedures to the design of the package itself and, whilst not being immediately ideal, we found that the cataloguing became an efficient process which was sufficiently flexible easily to accept additional entries, classes of object, and additional historical information.

Conservation

The cataloguing process also provides an opportunity to record the condition of the artefacts that the Abbey possesses. We are grateful to Tyne & Wear Archives & Museums for helping us with reviews of the state of the Abbey collection. A number of important conservation activities have taken place over the last three years during the project. These include stabilizing the Ogle chantry-chapel paintings, conserving the 1611 'Breeches' Bible, and the full cleaning and conservation of the Georgian Royal Coat of Arms at the west end of the Abbey. These three items had suffered over the years and we now know, to a much better extent, their constructional details and also their vulnerability. New display cases, bought as part of this Heritage Lottery Funded Project, ensure that the Bible is securely maintained in the correct atmosphere and that the regularly-changed temporary displays also receive their proper care.

Humidity and temperature measurements in the Abbey and near sensitive items in the exhibition also ensure that metalwork is kept at a low humidity and organic materials are kept in their ideal environment.

Conservation doesn't simply occur indoors — we have in the past 18 months found enough of the stones from the demolished Eastern Chapels, which faced the marketplace in Hexham, to enable a reconstruction of parts of the windows to show what we lost in

---

[3] "HEXAB" registered with The Collection Trust as the catalogue-number prefix unique to Hexham Abbey.

1858.[4] This was an unexpected benefit from the inspiration that this project has engendered.

A tribute must be paid to the staff and volunteers who have made this conservation management project viable, giving up their valuable free time. We have expertise available from a genealogist, a librarian, a historian, an IT specialist, an archaeologist, a senior National Trust museum conservator, and many others with varied experience. Well over twenty volunteers have been involved at one stage or another in creating the catalogue and providing advice.

The conservation part of the project has also thrown up many exciting new areas of the Abbey inventory. For example, wrapped in a duster at the back of a safe, a Russian Eastern Orthodox Church icon [Fig.2],[5] depicting the life of Christ, was brought to light again. When it was on display, one visitor recognized its importance and we now have been informed of a lot more detail about this item which had previously lain unseen for many years. Another example was the review of the prayer books and historical documents that were kept in a top cupboard in the vestry. Detailed examination and knowledgeable comment by a member of the retired clergy has allowed us to delight in the language and thoughts of pre-Victorian and even pre-Georgian prayer books.[6]

Simple cleaning and recording of everyday objects has also revealed some most interesting facts; for example, there are a number of cane-backed chairs in the Abbey which on examination were found to have come from Bohemia — probably before the First World War. These bent-wood chairs were not found in the manufacturer's catalogue and we believe them to be notable.

Some items appear quite unexpectedly. Replacement of the floorboards in the chancel choir stalls revealed many Abbey service cards which had been used for sketching by bored choristers, some dating back to the First World War. The quality of some drawings was astounding and they also revealed the usual furtive messaging between the choir stalls. But it gave comfort to those who say that the world is no better place or worse place now, as messages to and fro between the choirboys is a timeless occupation — as several ex-chorister visitors have attested. The cards also, it seemed, had a regular educational use to complete long division or French homework!

---

[4] See Chapter 5, page 37 et seq.
[5] HEXAB2138.
[6] See Chapter 7, page 59 et seq.

Fig.2: Russian Orthodox icon

The photography mentioned previously has also allowed us to update our knowledge of the many mason's marks which are numerous around the Abbey, as well as the ledger-stones and gravestones on the floor throughout the Abbey. Apart from previously documented ledger-stones in the chancel and transepts, there are many initials carved into the stonework of the walls and floor; these are believed to record burial places beneath the floor.

Another tribute to be paid at this stage is to Mr Colin Dallison. Much of the additional knowledge that is incorporated both in the archive — in a new archive room — and in the catalogue itself has been due to the patient recording and collating over many years of any detail about the Abbey that might prove relevant in the future. Colin's work was recognized by the Abbey in awarding him the title of Guardian of Hexham Abbey — and his continuing interest and additional information is proving to be invaluable in answering questions concerning the Abbey and its history.

Spreading the News

Communication is by definition a giving and receiving, and isn't necessarily limited to one direction. One of our developments in the conservation team is to ensure that an annual series of talks is held every January describing exciting and interesting discoveries on aspects of conservation. Another area is in the presentation of the Abbey story and its history to interested groups around Northumberland. The feedback from these events is often very illuminating.

But the process also works from visitors to the conservation group. A simple file on the visitors' book table has collected most interesting facts from passers-by. We now know, for example, who donated the large bookcase by the vestry; we know something of baptism stories going back to the time of Canon Savage; we know of choirboys' activities in the '60s, and many other fascinating stories. These have been reviewed in the Abbey News & Views and have also been the subject of one of our January talks. We are most grateful to our visitors for helping us discover more about the history of the Abbey, its people, and its collection.

Another aspect of communication concerns our relations with other museums. We have mentioned the Northumberland Archive at Woodhorn with whom we have regular contact. We also talk with Durham Cathedral and York Minster and their conservation teams, and have learned a lot from them. One other discussion we have had recently is with the Hamilton Kerr Institute, part of the Fitzwilliam Museum in Cambridge. They are experts in English panel painting and have been most helpful and interested in what we have here in Hexham — one of the finest collections of medieval 15th-century panel paintings in Britain. Our researchers have also discovered items in other museums' collections that have at some time been associated with Hexham. The V&A have several items of medieval embroidery that have a reputed Hexham history[7] and the British Museum, of course, has more than one artefact from Hexham in its collection, e.g. the silver plaque showing the image of a saint, of which we have a fine replica displayed in The Big Story Exhibition [Fig.3][8].

Fig.3: Early Christian Silver Plaque, replica

Communication with museums also includes the most helpful support we have had from members of the Conservation Panel. This panel — equivalent to Board of Trustees in an accredited museum — has benefited enormously from the contributions from Professor Richard Bailey, a nationally-recognized archaeologist and of Dr. Robert Collins of Newcastle University. Dr Collins was very helpful in getting a number of Anglo-Saxon coins from the Hexham Hoard [Fig.4] returned on long-term loan for the new exhibition, and we are most grateful to these two gentlemen in particular for their time and to support. We are also grateful for the good sense

---

[7] See Chapter 8, page 78 et seq.
[8] HEXAB2098.

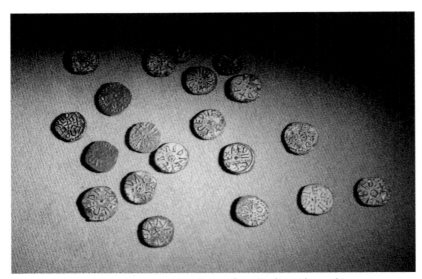

Fig.4: Stycas from the Hexham hoard

and guidance from Dr Stan Beckensall, a well-known local expert in pre-Christian and Northumbrian archaeology.

Mention must be made of contributions from members of the public at home and overseas, both of information and of physical objects. The objects range from previously unknown books and artwork to a beautiful silver brooch [Fig.5][9], dating from circa 1889, that we were offered in 2014 by an Australian lady who had come across it in Tasmania. We have also received from a parishioner a calendar for 1957 showing pictures of Hexham Abbey that we never knew existed. We've had donations of pictures of HM the Queen taken during her visit in 1974 that were also new to us and we are grateful for all the contributions made. We have been exhibiting recently a most interesting hieroglyphic bible dating from the 18th century which was donated by a local family.

The Abbey Exhibition area

Mention must be made of the quite remarkable success of the new exhibition area.[10] A small group, headed by the then Rector, Canon Graham Usher, and Mrs Toni Bush, developed a vision of what could be shown to a wide range of visitors. Writing a brief description of the Roman presence in Hexham, the travels of St.

---

[9] HEXAB2126.
[10] See Chapter 3, page 21 et seq.

Fig.5: Silver brooch with "Hexham Abbey"

Wilfrid, or the difficult history of the medieval period in eighty words, and designed to appeal to both young and old, whilst retaining factual integrity, was no easy task. A number of people bent their minds to this with great success — and very little argument! The exhibition shows some of the Abbey treasures — the Saxon chalice, the medieval passion painting sequence and the aforementioned Anglo-Saxon coins and stones.

Computer graphics[11] show the development of the Abbey church from its inception in 674 to the present day as well as indicating the possible use and location of its unique stone treasures. There are also interesting hand-on exhibits that have proved resilient to small hands. Even dressing up clothes have survived well! Grandparents seem to enjoy instructing their small charges in the process of how to construct an abbey without use of the internal combustion engine.

Good Fortune

The conservation portion of the HLF Project has benefited from being allowed a wide scope for its activities, relatively un-constrained by the normal procedures or organization of the Parish. This has assisted the examination and recording of the Abbey

---

[11] See Chapter 9, page 81 *et seq.*

history and artefacts according to the particular skills and interests of each of its volunteer staff. This in turn has led to a very high quality patchwork quilt of records and information to pass on to the next generation.

Another piece of good fortune has been the local academic environment. With a wealth of Roman history and the legacy of the early Christian northern church, the northeast corner of England has a strong cultural interest in its area. This has led to the aforementioned support of the Universities in the area, the encouragement of the local history societies, and a steady supply of interested retired specialists. Assistance and advice from staff at local English Heritage sites also helped us in the early days of planning and, particularly, cataloguing.

What Next?

The conservation group is examining the potential for obtaining accredited-museum status for the exhibition area and for the care of the Abbey collection. There are number of benefits to this. The first is that it will provide a driver to ensure the future good management of the Abbey collection. It will also give comfort to any organization that plans to offer an exhibit for a temporary display in the Abbey spaces. It will also provide greater opportunities for grant aid to ensure the proper care of the collection. The conservation team and the Conservation Advisory Group members are committed to: ensuring that we know what we have in the Abbey; continuing to learn and communicate the Hexham Abbey story; and ensuring that the items in our care are safeguarded for future generations.

2. What If...?
150 Years of Proposed Extensions to the Abbey

Chris Britton

By the end of the 19th century it was considered that the Abbey was becoming too small for the growing needs of the population of the town, while by the middle of the 20th century a demand for facilities beyond those of worship had begun to emerge. This chapter offers a summary of the various schemes that were proposed to deal with these demands. While few actually came to fruition, they provide an interesting commentary on the changing attitudes to the development and conservation of historic places of worship over the past century and a half.

At the dissolution of the Priory in 1537 the monastic buildings were sold off to function as a manor house, and the monastic choir, eastern chapels, transepts, crossing, and tower became the parish church. The site of the unfinished nave became a graveyard. This situation remained unchanged until the second half of the 19th century.

Fig.6: The 1870 vestry extension on the left, on the site of the medieval nave

11

In 1870 a new vestry was built, effectively recreating one bay of the lost nave, and probably qualifying as the tallest ever vestry — the full 65ft height of the former nave [Fig.6].[1] However, this was to

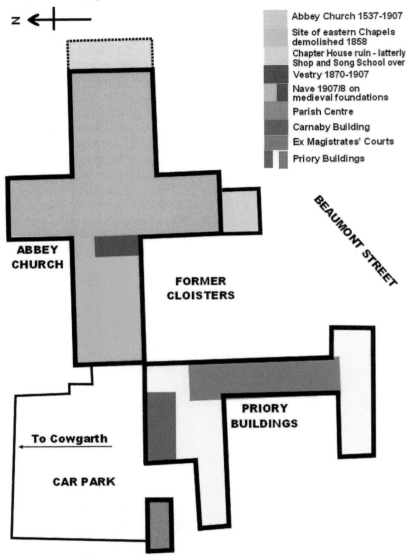

Fig.7: Block plan of Abbey church & priory buildings

[1] photo: Gibson, NRO 1876/C6/06.

be short lived as in 1899, under the direction of the new energetic Rector, E. Sidney Savage, a campaign was begun to rebuild the nave. The eminent late-Victorian Gothic-Revival architect, Temple Moore, was called in to work with the resident architect, C. C. Hodges.

Together they drew up a report on the state of the Abbey, and Moore prepared a plan for a new nave. It is known that this was in the 'Perpendicular' style[2] but sadly no copy of the plan has yet come to light. He also proposed recreating the eastern chapels [Fig.8],[3] which had been demolished in 1858.[4] The proposal to rebuild these chapels prompted very strong objections from one

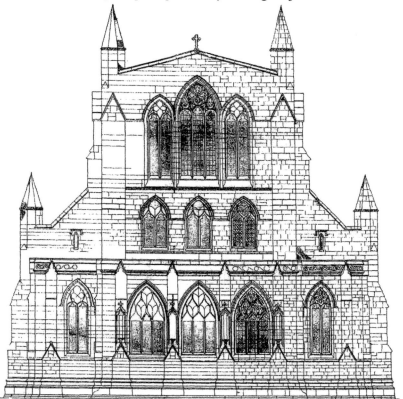

Fig.8: Moore's proposed east end with the chapels recreated

---

[2] Brandwood 1997, p.134.
[3] after Jennings 2001, p.61.
[4] See Chapter 5, page 37 et seq.

individual. This eventually led to the financial backer of the scheme withdrawing his offer[5] and the whole process ground to a halt. Nonetheless the proposals did make it as far as a planning application, but were shelved in view of the controversy. Quite what use the parish church would have had for another five chapels is a moot point, unless it was intended to use the space as vestries and a song school for the choir. It would be another 80 years before these facilities were provided.

In 1905 another attempt was made to rebuild the nave, and four alternative plans were drawn up. Two were by Moore: one in the Early English style to match the existing medieval church and which was not much liked, the other in the Decorated style which was what was eventually built. Hodges drew up the other two plans but sadly nothing further is known about them.[6]

At the same time an ambitious suggestion was made by Temple

Temple Moore, F.R.I.B.A.

Fig.9: Temple Moore's proposed vestries and museum adjoining the south transept

---

[5] Jennings 2001, p.59.
[6] Brandwood op cit.

Moore to recreate part of the monastic buildings adjoining the south transept.[7] This would have incorporated the ruins of the Chapter House and beyond, to provide additional vestry space at first floor level and a museum on the ground floor [Fig.9].[8] These developments were never implemented.

Subsequent proposals through the 20th century mostly relate to increasing vestry space (presumably for the choir?) and other facilities. In 1949, for example, plans were made for vestries on the

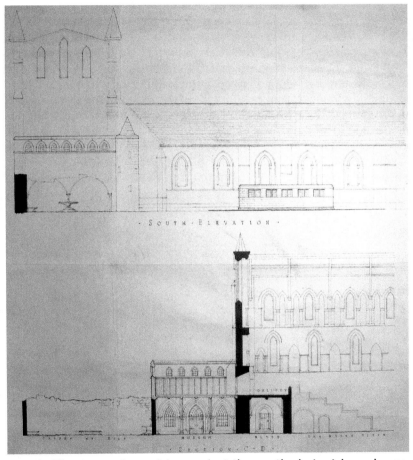

Fig.10: Plan to create vestries against the south choir aisle and song school over the chapter house vestibule, 1949

---

[7] Savage and Hodges 1907, pp.25–26.

south side of the chancel, and for a museum in the ruins of the Chapter House and a Song School above [Fig.10].[9] These came to nothing.

1949 also saw the emergence of a much more ambitious plan. This envisaged the reacquisition of the Priory Buildings, with the exception of the part used as the Magistrates' Courts; see block plan [Fig.7]. The southern wing fronting the park was to become a new Rectory, and involved taking a 26-foot-wide strip from the adjacent park right down to Beaumont Street to provide a garden for the Rector. This was to be screened from the cloister area by an openwork gothic screen — a poor man's version of the famous 'Wilkins' screen fronting The High at King's College, Cambridge? On the first floor of the northern wing a flat was to be provided for the curate, and below it a Parish Centre with Library in the part now occupied by the café and exhibition. At the western end of this wing on the ground floor were to be facilities for the Scouts and a link to a large and lofty new Parish Hall complete with a stage and all mod cons on the site of the present Parish Office and the western half of the car park [Fig.11].[10] This was all dressed in late Gothic garb, presumably to blend in with the Abbey. Were there any realistic

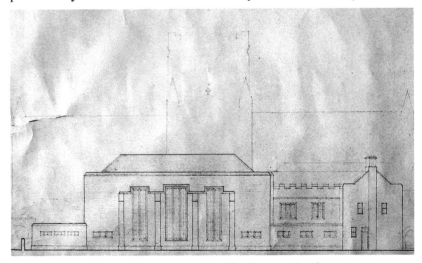

Fig.11: The 1949 proposed hall looking east: the existing north wing of the priory buildings on the right and the outline of the west view of the Abbey church behind

[8] after Savage & Hodges 1907, Plate XIV.
[9] HEXAB3222.1.
[10] from HEXAB3245.3.

Fig.12: The 1964 proposal for a modern style hall in car park at
the west end of the church looking south-west

chances of regaining these buildings at this time, let alone finding
the funds in the era of post-war austerity?

In 1961 there was another, much more modest proposal to
provide further facilities space by building a modern, relatively low,
hall on the grass area fronting Cowgarth between the Priory Gate
and the current Abbey car park, but again it came to nothing. Three
years later a more ambitious plan for a large 'Parish Centre' was
proposed, in a style typical of the period, in the same position as the
1949 hall [Fig.12].[11] This would probably now be considered a
wholly inappropriate design for such a sensitive site.

The Chapter House vestibule ruin had been restored in 1955, as
a single-storey building, and used as St Cuthbert's Chapel, not as
vestries or a museum as previously intended. The idea of building a
new Song School was again revisited in 1978 with a proposal to
build over St Cuthbert's Chapel, which itself was to be converted
into the Abbey Shop. This looked surprisingly similar in style to the
1949 scheme[12] but with an added spiral stair turret [Fig.13].[13]
Perhaps this was intended for after-hours access when the church
would be locked, or as a fire escape. By 1981 this scheme had
morphed into the building we know today but without the spiral
stair turret. The detailing of the earlier proposals were perhaps more
interesting than that which was finally built, but the pitched roof we
now have is certainly more in keeping with the Abbey, and
doubtless provides a more resonant acoustic in the Song School.

---

[11] HEXAB3247.1.
[12] See Fig.10 on page 1.
[13] HEXAB3228.

Fig.13: The 1978 song school proposal

Later proposals for extensions all relate to the provision of facilities considered vital to the running and maintenance of a place as historic and active as the Abbey in the 21st century: museum, café, halls, meeting rooms, offices and, most importantly, toilets! As recently as 2007 plans were drawn up to recreate the cloisters in a modern form which would also include reopening the door to the south transept and relocating the Flavinus monument. The east side of these cloisters was to be an exhibition space and shop extension, the north side a café, and the west side an education suite; the south side was to be a covered walkway. The scheme also included the Carnaby Building and the northern range of the Priory Buildings. In addition, a narthex was proposed against the west front of the Abbey Church to provide a porch and the all-important toilets.

However, these proposals in total proved to be too ambitious when the present HLF-funded project was formally initiated. The narthex proposal was dropped and the development in the cloister was limited to a linking porch in the north-west corner. Plans drawn in 2011 included only the northern range of the former Prior's House, plus the Carnaby Building and the Monastic Workshop (ground-floor only). The remainder of the Prior's eastern range was still occupied by the Magistrates' Court (which had closed 1st April 2011) and associated facilities, including the main staircase. Clearly it would be impractical to share this staircase with whoever took ownership of the court facilities, so where could one insert a stair and lift into such historic fabric? The proposal in 2011 was an interesting semi-elliptical stair wrapped around a lift shaft in what is

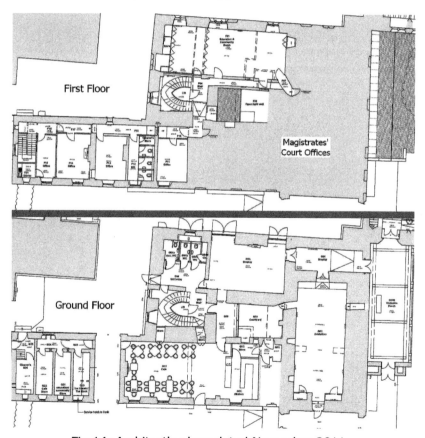

Fig.14: Architect's plans dated November 2011

now the Café's Allendale Room [Fig.14].[14] Similar plans in early 2012 had a much simpler staircase design with less impact on the historic fabric.

Later in 2012 the Abbey decided to raise additional funding and purchase the courtroom, and associated offices, so the project could be revised substantially. Although the main stair was now available the acquisition of the former ballroom (latterly the Magistrates' Court) provided a major facility which really needed a better staircase. The lightwell between the Carnaby Building and the former Prior's quarters was cleared of assorted sheds and other late additions, a glazed roof was provided, and the splendid staircase we now have was inserted with minimal impact on the historic fabric.

Perhaps it is fortunate that none of the earlier proposals came to fruition, otherwise who knows what would have happened to the Priory Buildings when they eventually became vacant in 2011? Their reunification with the Abbey after nearly 500 years has not only provided all the facilities the Abbey could wish for, but saved them from inappropriate use or dereliction.

---

[14] from HEXAB5100.

3. The Adaptation of the Priory Buildings

Chris Cotton

Introduction

The bringing together of the Priory Church with the former monastic priory buildings has been led by a careful and sensitive process of spatial reintegration, that has now established anew, a single ecclesiastical complex to serve the life and mission of the church, the community, and all who visit Hexham Abbey. It has also added coherence to the understanding and enjoyment of the heritage. The long separation of church from the monastic buildings began at the dissolution of the monastery in *circa* 1536, following which the Priory Church became the Parish Church and ranges of monastic buildings, courts, and precincts were transferred into private, then eventual public, ownership. During this extended interregnum both Priory Church and former monastic buildings have continued to separately develop, adapting to changes in use, as well as to new uses. The wider physical context of what was formerly the extended Priory Precincts and enclosures has also changed, as the town of Hexham and its public spaces have evolved. This process of inevitable change has introduced a richness and 'layering' to the heritage and significance of the buildings and their setting, which is now an integral part of the place.

The integration of the Priory Church and monastic buildings into a single complex acknowledges continuity within the process of change. The appropriation of the former monastic buildings and spaces into single Hexham Abbey ownership has not been a process of restoration of a bygone age. It has been one of creative conservation, that has brought new use and life in such a way that the layers of historical development of the buildings, their significance, and the people who cared for the buildings, can be more readily understood and enjoyed. The acquisition and adaptation of the monastic buildings adds another chapter to the unfolding story of Hexham Abbey, and opens the page to the next episode.

The collaborative design process between client, led by Canon Graham Usher, Toni Bush, Tom Kelsey, and John Robinson, architect, consultants, and advisors, organized the competing objectives and advice to achieve a complementary design solution that is functional to use, beautiful to experience, and coherent with respect to the complex historical layering of the monastic and later buildings. The conservation philosophy adopted ensured primary archaeological material and building fabric has been retained, significance enhanced, and interventions made reversible.

The strategic project aims included primarily addressing the pressing need for space and facilities for members of the Abbey Community to fulfil more effectively their activities; to improve their welcome, access, use, and understanding of the Abbey for all who visit; to understand the significance of the buildings and their capacity for change; to address the conservation need for the buildings with respect to programmes of repair; and to establish sustainable revenue streams.

Hexham Abbey, like many greater parish churches, is of the scale and complexity of a cathedral church. However, it had no 'secular' space or dedicated facilities for hospitality, display and interpretation, educational activities, archive and collections storage, and multi-purpose events and meeting spaces. The offer to the community was limited, and the lack of space compromised the life, mission, and activities of the church and community.

The framework for understanding the historical development and significances of the priory buildings, together with their capacity for change and conservation need, was explained through the Conservation Management Plan, prepared by Jane Gibson. This underpinned and guided the strategic planning of the spaces and identified beneficial opportunities for change.

In general terms, there are four key phases of historic development within the priory and later buildings around which the spatial planning of the design proposal is organized. First, the medieval structures of the monastic priory buildings and archaeological remains, principally comprising the claustral west range, Prior's Lodging, and Priory Church. Second, the fortified house built for Sir Reynold Carnaby, *circa* 1539. Third, the interior rehabilitation and gentrification of the whole complex by Diana Beaumont, John Dobson architect, and others during the 19th century. Fourth, the Abbey Church and the completion of the Nave and western entrances in *circa* 1908 by The Revd Sidney Savage and Temple Moore, architect.

The initial design concept was tested through consultation with the conservation officers, Historic England, the Diocesan Advisory Committee, and the County Archaeologist, following which a series of below- and above-ground archaeological and building investigations were made by Peter Ryder[1] and Richard Carlton. This enabled the concept design to be refined, incorporating the findings and advice, and formal consents sought for statutory approval. As the design development and building works unfolded on site, consultation, investigation, and collaboration continued.

The Cloister Porch

The design objective to ensure that the new facilities within the priory buildings should all be accessible and connected under a single roof to the Abbey Church by a new Cloister Porch was a key consideration. The Abbey Church is seen as the primary asset, and the new facilities complement and complete, rather than compete with it. The concept for a Cloister Porch was developed; this new structure provides a useful gathering space from both the Abbey Church interior, as well as a useable entry from the external Cloister Garth and town. The exterior appearance of sandstone and Westmoreland slate is restrained and sympathetic to the celebrated surrounding buildings, its open doors provide a welcome into an uplifting space, appropriate to the entry of the great church. The new footings and floor structure were carefully calculated following the archaeological trials to ensure historic remains were retained *in situ*. The floor level of the Porch is above that of the Nave, and a new ramp and step arrangement in the western bay of the Nave creates ramped level access between the two spaces, whilst also forming a 'gallery' for those witnessing the Baptismal Rite at the Font [Fig.15]. The interior form and structure of the new porch was shaped to fully expose within the space the moulded stone reveal of the *circa* 15th-century southwest door of the Nave. Temple Moore's forbidding external oak door was relocated to form the secure external south door of the new porch, and a new glazed door installed in the historic arch, providing the visitor on arrival into the space with an inviting glimpse into the church and the canopy over the Font. The internal green oak structural frame continues the great tradition of carpentry at Hexham Abbey. Archaeological investigation into a blocked medieval door opening in the east wall of the west claustral range confirmed that this could be reopened, reinstating a once important link, so that access from the Cloister Porch could be made into the Priory and Carnaby Buildings.

---

[1] See Chapter 4, page 29 *et seq.*

Fig.15: The Abbey church new access
into the cloister porch

Medieval Monastic Priory Buildings

Passing into the medieval Priory Buildings from the Cloister Porch, one is immediately within the medieval stone rib-vaulted undercroft spaces of the west claustral range. These monastic undercroft storage spaces are formed of massive stone construction; as such they provide a stable internal environment with high potential for thermal buffering that is also physically secure. They are a good choice for the new exhibition and displays where security and a stable environment are paramount. To achieve a stable interior environment, works were carried out to address problems of damp and ground water ingress. The first stage included remedial works to ensure the external drainage and ground water disposal was operating. The building was then repointed in lime mortars to improve the breathability of the building so that moisture can be more readily dispersed from the building fabric rather than be confined in the wall to excessive levels by the cement mortars. The programme of full repointing was extended to all the buildings. The non-breathable modern floor coverings were removed, revealing a river cobble and York-stone flag floor. The historic floor could not be used as the accessible levels were not achievable and the old floor was protected and retained *in situ*, with a new breathable limecrete floor with underfloor heating installed. To the south end of the larger space a new environmental heating and dehumidification system has been installed to further support the formation of a stable interior environment. The architecture of these early monastic spaces are as much a part of the exhibition as are the treasures and displays, and help tell the story of the monastic use of the priory.

The range of buildings that were formerly the Prior's Lodging were thought to have been substantially rebuilt during the 19th century following two devastating fires in 1797 and 1818. The archaeological investigations, particularly within the ground floor room, exposed the fire-back, hearth and part of the carved and moulded stone jamb of a 15th-century fire-place. Adjacent to this, a medieval window opening was discovered which looked into what would have been the western entry court of the Priory. Both of these features were felt to be of such significance to the understanding of the former Prior's Lodging, that they are now revealed within the new café. This provides an appropriate time link to the hospitality once offered by the Prior to visitors, and those visiting the Abbey today. The discovery of these features in this wall suggest more of the medieval structure was retained following the fires than had previously been thought.

Sir Reynold Carnaby's Fortified House

Sir Reynold Carnaby's House comprised a two-storey L-shaped building that infilled the north western area between the two medieval monastic ranges, forming a small inner courtyard space. This building, complete with substantial timber floors and roofs survived the two great fires, so largely remained intact. However, the process of 19th-century gentrification and 20th-century public use, had led to many of the spaces such as the courtyard and large first-floor reception hall becoming infilled with partitioning and construction, very little of it being of high heritage value, but much of it disguising the extraordinarily interesting Carnaby building.

A key design challenge was identifying an appropriate location for the proposed new stair [Fig.16]. The removal of the accumulated low grade building clutter in the open courtyard restored the original proportions and revealed details of the space, such as the three garderobe windows, decorative carved Roman-style cornice, the remains of a circular tower stair between first floor and roof level. A new glazed roof continues the top-lit courtyard, and a new easy-going modern stair, clearly separated from the historic walls, continues the idea of open court space. The paring back of modern plasters and construction revealed on every wall surface the antiquity and detail of this unique building.

Fig.16: The courtyard of Sir
Reynold Carnaby's house

The previously hidden garderobes, infilled during the 18th and 19th centuries were opened up, as were the carved and dressed stone chimney and fire reveals, to explain the design and character of Carnaby's building. Following considerable thought, later separating 19th-century partitions were removed; the benefits being the formation of a single large education and multi-purpose space which reinstates the proportions of Sir Reynold's principal first-floor room and looks across the former entry precinct of the Priory.

The reopening of blocked doorways within the courtyard has enabled this space to be the circulation hub that connects the ground-floor display spaces with the new restaurant facilities, and events and education facilities on the first floor.

Diana Beaumont's gentrified interiors

Following the two devastating fires that damaged much of the west claustral range and Prior's Lodging, many of the spaces were rehabilitated and gentrified with simple but elegant interiors. These works included the formation of new timber sash windows with panelled and shuttered reveals, cornices, dados, new fire surrounds, and a decorative scheme, now lost. Much of this interior is retained within the repaired buildings. One room that has been restored is the former ballroom on the first floor formed within the former lay brothers' dormitory of the claustral west range. This space had been subdivided into three spaces during its latter use as the Court Room, and much of its elegant plastered ceiling was hidden. Removing the modern partitions, conserving the historic ceiling, repairing the walls, and introducing new heating, ventilation, and lighting systems has brought this room back into use as an exceptional events space. Beneath its gentrified surfaces remain the archaeology of the medieval priory building, the stone vaulted floor structure and the stone stair passage leading down into the cloisters.

There have been many great moments and events in the long history of Hexham Abbey that have transformed its buildings and its life. The bringing together of Hexham Abbey with the former priory buildings, in such a way that adds to the enthralling story of the place and the understanding of its heritage, is one of those moments that will be a transforming benefit to the Abbey, the

Fig.17: Diana Beaumont's restored ballroom

community, and all who visit this very special place. This moment was marked by the Blessing of the new facilities by the Bishop of Newcastle, The Rt Revd Martin Wharton on his last visit to Hexham Abbey as Bishop, following his 17 years of devoted service to the diocese and region.

4. Discoveries in the Abbey House during the 2013/4 Works

Peter F Ryder

The name 'Abbey House' has been applied to the group of buildings attached to the south-west corner of Hexham Abbey church, which have their origin in the west range of the conventual buildings of the medieval Augustinian Priory, along with further ranges that once enclosed a courtyard on its west side. These buildings, extended and remodelled, formed a manorial residence from the Dissolution until the early 19th century, after which they passed to a variety of secular uses. In 2013 most of the group was returned to the church, and converted for use as a visitor centre; archaeological recording during this conversion revealed many interesting features and shed much light on a complex history

The principal components of the group referred to in the following account, are the West Range in which the ground floor of the medieval cloister range survives, the so-called Prior's House Range projecting west to form the north side of Prior's Court, and the Carnaby Building. Built by Sir Reynold Carnaby in 1539, this latter structure formed an L-plan block in the angle between the West Range and the north side of the Prior's House Range and enclosed what is here termed the Small Court.

Discoveries in the West Range.

At the north end of the range is a former through passage whose eastern doorway had been blocked in *c.*1800 and concealed by re-facing on the east (cloister) face of the wall. As part of the 2013/14 works this doorway [A][1] was re-opened [Fig.19] and the passage re-floored. The doorway has some claim to be the earliest above-ground architectural feature at Hexham; of simple Romanesque style, it has been associated with the foundation of the Augustinian Priory by Archbishop Thomas II of York in 1113. Eric Cambridge[2] has pointed out that it is closely paralleled in the late-11th-century monastic buildings at Jarrow, and to have pre-dated the construction of any west range. Facing west, it has rebated jambs of simple square section, with a drawbar tunnel and socket, carrying a lintel

---

[1] Letters [A]...[Y] are marked on Fig.18, page 1.
[2] Cambridge & Williams, 1995, p.83.

that has a trapezoidal key block, beneath a blind tympanum under a semicircular arch.

The passage itself has a vault carried on seven segmental-arched and casement-moulded ribs; its north wall is complex, with three phases of fabric pre-dating the upper courses (which seem to go with the vault), whereas on the south the wall seems a single build, with a central shoulder-arched doorway that might have been re-used from elsewhere. At the west end of the passage is a westward-facing doorway [B], shown as blocked on Hodge's 1888

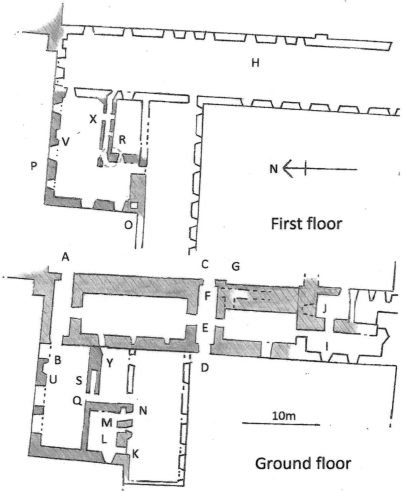

Fig.18: Floor plans of the western monastic range (blue) and Carnaby House (red)

Fig.19: Doorway [A] when exposed
during the archaeological work

plan[3] and on a 1903 plan[4] but reopened by 1913.[5] It has a steep two-centred arch, and was again protected by a drawbar tunnel.

South of the passage is the so-called Monastic Workshop, now housing the main exhibition, where the removal of recent floors and a cross wall of uncertain date revealed an older slabbed central walkway flanked by neat cobbling, with evidence of removed structures, perhaps wine bins. Several features of the floor suggested that it was of no great age, and had been cut down below the medieval levels. Three openings in the western wall were

---

[3] Hodges, 1888, Plate 55.
[4] Durham District Land Registry ND 111451.
[5] Hodges, 1913, fold-out Plan A opp. p.8.

originally windows, several employing medieval cross-slabs as lintels. Between the fifth and six ribs of the vault are the remains of a stair leading down from the room above. Stopping somewhat short of the floor, this was presumably originally completed by a ladder. At the southern end of this chamber a door, now obscured by the set of Passion Paintings, led into the central passage.

The central passage, which now allows open access from the cloister into the Prior's Court, formerly opened from the cloister by an early round-headed arch, shown as blocked on a 1783 drawing by Samuel Hieronymus Grimm.[6] The present doorway [C] seems to be a 19th-century copy of the 13th-century one at the west end [D], which, together with the side walls of the passage, seem to predate the present segmental vault carried on seven transverse chamfered ribs; set at a lower level at the western corners are the springers for an earlier vault.

On the south side of the passage is a post-medieval doorway [E] into the southern undercroft (which was not involved in the 2013/2014 works), with at the east end of the wall a blocked shoulder-arched doorway [F] which originally gave access to a mural stair rising to the south. This was probably the original access to the hall on the first floor, but had been long sealed off, though a section of the stair [G] could be examined by removing the blocking from a small window opening on to the cloister walk. A brick wall on the north sealed off a stair-foot lobby, from which there was presumably a doorway into the southern undercroft whilst to the south, 1.3 m away, was a stone blocking. In between were three steps of the stair, and a roof which rose in corresponding steps as well, with an oversailing hollow-chamfered course on the west wall, and neat chamfered edges to the risers. The topmost of the roof slabs was a re-used medieval grave slab with roll-moulded angles and an incised pair of shears. The head of the stair, where its uppermost steps turned at ninety degrees to the west to enter the upper chamber [H], was seen during floor works in the Courtroom.

South of the stair, the westernmost bay of the frater undercroft unusually overlapped the cloister to extend into the west range and now forms a boiler room, roofed by a post-medieval brick vault. Removal of render showed the south wall to be a brick-and-timber partition, perhaps of the 18th century, but the west wall proved to be medieval and had a doorway with a pointed arch [I], and an integral wall rib of the original vault. There were also remains of northward-

---

[6] Hodges, 1924 Plate XIII; Cambridge & Williams, 1995, p.86.

facing four-centred doorway [J] in the north wall, which was better seen in the underfloor works in the Courtroom, from which it was evident that the 14th-century east wall of the west range butted up against the earlier 1.8-metre-thick north wall of the frater. This doorway must have opened from a lobby to the south of the mural stair.

Discoveries in the Prior's House

The "Prior's House Range" is, in its present form, a late-18th/early-19th-century building, broadly replicating the form of its predecessor, with an arched entry where old illustrations show a medieval gatehouse. All that survives of the earlier structure is the section of its north wall that was abutted externally by the Carnaby Building — however, this proved to contain a wealth of interesting features. On the ground floor were remains of a medieval (15th-century?) moulded fireplace [K], which probably originally had a four-centred arch. To the east of the fireplace was a splayed window [L] and then an inserted passage [M] through into the Carnaby Building, with a re-used medieval cross slab as its lintel. The remains of a second window [N] lay to the east. To the west of the fireplace there appeared to have been a shaft, presumably once provided with a ladder, up into a tiny Watch Chamber at first-floor level [O], formed within the projection of the stack backing the ground-floor fireplace. This had little loops to north and west, overlooking the external face of the former gateway to the west, which would have enabled a surreptitious surveillance of any visitors before they were permitted to enter.

Discoveries in the Carnaby Building

The finds made here, while removing late-20th-century fittings and accretions suffered when the building was used by the local Social Services department, allowed this interesting building to be properly understood for the first time. When Sir Reynold Carnaby became bailiff and general administrator, he was a man under threat, and in 1539 built himself what was very much a self-contained strong house; its defensive nature had not been previously appreciated. It is a building of some quality, constructed of newly-quarried stone rather than re-used material from surplus monastic buildings (as might have been expected). Its north wall was adorned with his coat of arms [P][Fig.20]. A re-examination of this showed

0   50cm

Fig.20: Sir Reynold Carnaby's coat of arms

significant differences from previously-published accounts.[7] In recognition of his services in campaigns against the Scots, Carnaby's crest had been augmented in 1534 from a simple Saracen's head to one with a 'sermet [cloth band] russet gould and tawny' tied round the temples, with three silver crescents on it and two silver 'tirretts' by his ear — ear rings which still remain, carved in stone but free-hanging, a remarkable survival.

Whilst commanding the outer court of the Abbey from its south-east corner, access into the house could only be gained by a convoluted route from the Prior's Court through the Prior's House and then into the Small Court. At the north-west corner of the court was the entrance door [Q], protected by an overhanging circular turret (which partially survived at roof level, [R]) in the re-entrant angle of the range [Fig.21]. Such was the isolation of the block that it was protected during both of the major fires that destroyed much of the medieval Abbey House. Carnaby's house was provided with at least four mural garderobe chambers, that adjoining the entrance lobby [S] being found to have survived intact when its doorway was

---

[7] Ryder, 2014, pp.27–31.

Fig.21: Interior view of turret [R] seen from below at the time of discovery

unblocked. Another at the south-east corner of the West Range had been cut through by the later passage [M], but its seat and chute remained [T], infilled with broken hollow-chamfered mullions identifiable as coming from the eastern of the first-floor windows on the north front, which the evidence of old prints show was destroyed between 1720 and 1778. The ground-floor chamber in the northern range retains a fine contemporary fireplace [U] but the large windows flanking it are relatively recent; originally the ground floor of the building only had narrow slits or cruciform loops (for guns?), shown in old prints [e.g. Fig.22];[8] larger windows were confined to the upper floor, and even here were provided with substantial external iron grilles.

On the upper floor, the main hall seems to have been in the North Range, and its splendid fireplace [V] was uncovered in 2011, with a smaller 18th-century successor installed within it. The mural passage in the south wall of the hall [X] seems to have been produced by knocking together two back-to-back garderobes (a triplet of exit chutes [Y], including that from the ground-floor garderobe, were seen at the foot of the wall). It is still unclear how the first floor rooms were arranged; there must have been a stair in the North Range, as the intact floor frames of the West Range

---

[8] Hodges, 1888, Plate 6.

Fig.22: An 18th-century view of the Carnaby House with the
adjoining gatehouse to the Priors' Court and surviving
monastic buildings

showed no sign of one. Another remarkable survival was that both
ranges retain their original roofs; that of the north range has six
trusses and that of the west three, all of truncated principal type with
two levels of through purlins, the common rafters being morticed
onto the ends of the saddle, and then pegged together at the apex.

Thus archaeological recording during the ongoing structural
works has enabled the conventual buildings of the medieval priory
— and their interesting post-medieval history — to be better
understood. The newly-revealed structural features of the Carnaby
Building, as explained here, illuminate the troubled mind of
Reynold Carnaby who chose to build himself a new residence to a
design which so emphasized security. Prior to the works it had been
thought that he might simply have re-fashioned an existing building,
but this now seems very unlikely to have been the case.
Archaeology and history for once successfully combine in telling its
story.

5. The Eastern Chapels Tracery Project

Chris Tolan-Smith

Destruction and Demolition

On Tuesday the 9th of September 1828 visitors to Hexham market found more to interest them than the occasional bargain, for on that day part of the east end of the Abbey church collapsed onto the group of buildings clustered around its foot. The most important of those buildings was a group of five chantry chapels. Throughout the 19th century and indeed more recently, this building has been referred to as the Lady Chapel. There is no evidence that this was actually ever the case and Hodges dismissed the idea entirely.[1] More correctly they should be referred to as the choir aisle or the Eastern Chapels, the term preferred here. This group of five chapels, under a single roof, had been built during the second quarter of the 14th century. After the Reformation they were converted to other uses, including at one time as a school and were still known as the 'Old School' in 1828. Also, over time a number of other buildings had accreted around them consisting of houses and retail premises. The collapse is thought to have been due to a structural weakness in the Abbey's east window which, in its then form, had been installed less than a century before.

John Dobson was called in to restore the Abbey's window and to carry out some temporary repairs to the chapels. By the 1840s plans were initiated for their full restoration and an appeal was launched by the Town Council. In circumstances that seem familiar in 2017, it was found necessary first to raise funds to purchase and then demolish the abutting houses and shops before work could start on the chapels themselves. In spite of the difficulty in raising the funds, this still seemed a realistic possibility in the early 1850s and the architect Robert W Billings was invited to draw up proposals for the restoration of the chapels [Fig.23].[2] In the event, while it eventually proved possible to remove the houses and shops, insufficient funds were left to deal with the chapels and in the words of Charles Clement Hodges the chapels were 'swept away in July 1858' as part of Dobson's whole scale 'restoration' of the east end of the Abbey church.[3]

---

[1] Hodges, 1919, p.111.
[2] HEXAB3227.
[3] Hodges, 1919, p.29.

Fig.23: Drawings of the chapels in 1852
and a proposed restoration

By the time Hodges arrived in Hexham in the 1870s nothing remained of Eastern Chapels other than a number of architectural fragments scattered around the Abbey grounds, in some cases being used to edge footpaths and flower beds. However, Hodges did have the benefit of several earlier drawings, including that produced by Billings [Fig.23] and, most importantly, a single photograph taken by Gibson in 1858 shortly before the chapels' demolition [Fig.24].[4]

---

[4] Hodges, 1888, Plate 7.

38

Fig.24: Gibson's 1858 photograph

With these to hand Hodges was able to reconstruct, on paper, the outlines of the chapels, details of which he then set out in his 1888 monograph [Fig.25].[5]

More recently the chapels have been the subject of a detailed study by Nicola Coldstream.[6] In summary, the building extended for 18.25m (60 feet) by 7.5m (25 feet) and rose to a ridge of 10.1m (33 feet). The long axis lay north-south across the full extent of the east end of the Abbey church. The Gibson photograph and the Billings

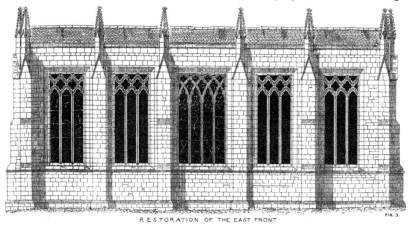

RESTORATION OF THE EAST FRONT

Fig.25: Hodges' 1888 reconstruction drawing of the east front

---

[5] Hodges, 1888, Plate 37.

drawing show that it was divided into five unequal bays separated by buttresses with crocketed pinnacles. The main, east, elevation had a window in each bay and there were single windows in both the north and south gable ends.

On the basis of the drawings and the Gibson photograph, it is clear that all seven windows were provided with tracery in the Decorated Style of the mid-14th century. They had certainly been built by 1350, for in that year the Archbishop of York granted the canons an extra five feet of ground in the market place so that they could continue to process around the outside of the Abbey.[7]

Recovery

In 2012, members of the Abbey's Conservation Group began to catalogue loose stone items lying within the church and in a corner of the Campy Hill graveyard, along with others demarcating the flower beds outside the parish office and in the grounds of Hexham House. Twelve months later 230 individual items had been catalogued including a wide range of different types. Notable items include important pieces of Anglo-Saxon sculpture, a series of medieval grave covers and stone coffins, liturgical items such as Holy-Water stoops and cresset stones, and numerous architectural fragments. The latter category includes column bases, capitals and shafts, moulded blocks, hood moulds, and architrave fragments. However, complete pieces and fragments of bar tracery form the most numerous category.

Bar tracery consists of moulded stone bars assembled to form patterns in a window head and usually including grooves to facilitate glazing. It was first developed in France during the earlier 13th century and became one of the defining features of both the Decorated and Perpendicular Styles of English church architecture. Dating from the late 13th century to the early 16th, a variety of increasingly complex styles developed.[8] However, even the apparently most complex designs can be analysed to show that they are based on the use of a few simple geometric figures; principally arcs, circles and ellipses.

No medieval examples of bar tracery survive *in situ* at Hexham, but at an early stage in cataloguing the stonework it became clear that a number of pieces of tracery could be re-assembled to give an

--------(cont.)--------

6 Coldstream, 1995.
7 Hodges, 1888, p.9.
8 Hart, 2012.

idea of a complete scheme of decoration. Moreover, it also became clear that this scheme could be matched in the Billings and Hodges drawings of the windows of the Eastern Chapels. Accordingly, the study of these fragments goes some way towards enabling the destroyed Eastern Chapels to take their 'rightful place on the map of Decorated buildings in Northumberland'.[9]

In its simplest form the tracery from the Eastern Chapels is made up of three elements which may be described as basically **V-shaped**, **Y-shaped**, and **X-shaped**. Modified versions of these forms provided the jambs and window head sections. Both the **Y-** and

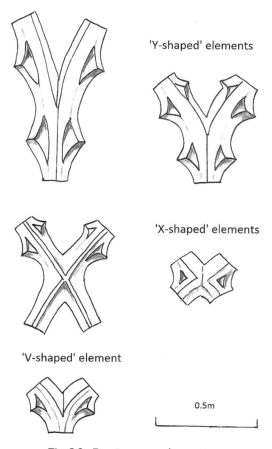

'Y-shaped' elements

'X-shaped' elements

'V-shaped' element

0.5m

Fig.26: Bar tracery elements

---

[9] Coldstream, 1995, p.99.

X-shaped elements come in two sizes, 'large' and 'small' [Fig.26].

A number of the **V-shaped** and **Y-shaped** elements have rectilinear grooves [Fig.27] cut transversely across their lower interfaces to accommodate wrought iron bars, indicating that these elements were the bottom components of the tracery schemes.

The outer pairs of windows on the east elevation are composed of **V-shaped** elements, ten in each window with four additional sections providing the jambs. With a total of four windows deploying **V-shaped** elements the total assemblage consisted of 40 such elements with 16 pieces to provide the jambs. These elements were assembled to form trefoiled heads to the three main lights of each window with similar but inverted trefoils at the head and a quatrefoil at the centre [Fig.25]. The pattern underlying this design is of 'reversed S-shaped' or ogival curves to create a net-like structure. Tracery assembled in this way is called **Reticulated Tracery.**

The Conservation Group have recovered 16 **V-shaped** elements and four jambs constituting the tracery from one-and-a-half of the windows of the east elevation [Fig.28].

The central window of the east elevation used both **Y-shaped** and **X-shaped** elements to provide the tracery at the head of its four lights. The complete window consisted of three main **Y-shaped** elements with half-elements either side to form the jambs which together provide cinquefoil heads to the lights. Above these large and small **X-shaped** elements completed the design to the window

Fig.27: Basal grooves

head forming elongated and squashed quatrefoils [Fig.25]. The

Fig.28: Re-assembled 'reticulations' from one window of the east elevation

pattern underlying this design is of parallel intersecting curves, a defining feature of the **Late Geometric Style**.

The Conservation Group have recovered 40% of the tracery from the central window [Fig.29].

Fig.29: Re-assembled tracery from the central window of the east elevation

The east elevation was recorded in both the Billings drawing of 1852 and the Gibson photograph of 1858. Neither featured the north gable, though this does appear in two drawings in the British Library dating from early 18th and early 19th centuries.[10] Hodges used these as the basis for his drawing [Fig.30].[11] There are no

Fig.30: Hodges 1888 reconstruction drawing of the windows in the north and south elevations

---

[10] King George III Topographical Collection [Shelfmark: K.Top. vol XXXII, Item number: 48b] and Grimm's Northumberland Sketches. See also Fig.32 on page 1.
[11] HEXAB3207.

records of what the south gable looked like, but Hodges assumed that it was the same. Unlike the windows of the east elevation, which were square headed, that in the north gable occupied a two-centred segmental arch. Also, the tracery continued some way below the springing of the arch and can be classified as **Drop Tracery**.

This window had five lights and the bottom section of tracery consisted on four **Y-shaped** elements with half-elements either side to form the jambs. These **Y-shaped** elements differ from those in the east elevation, having a shorter distance between the cusps, 280mm (11 inches) as opposed to 380mm (15 inches). They provided cinquefoil heads to the five lights of the window. Above, a bank of five small **X-shaped** elements provided a link with four further, but inverted, **Y-shaped** elements. These defined a row of four quatrefoils and then continued the design to the window head incorporating three trefoils. The underlying design is of intersecting arcs with radii of 3 foot 6 inches (1.1m). The result is a series of ogival curves, a characteristic feature of the **Curvilinear Style.**

So far parts of five bottom elements from this scheme have been identified. Like those from the central window of the east elevation, they have grooves in their lower interfaces. It is also the case, that elements from this window have small roughly incised crosses on their interfaces, a feature absent from the central window of the east elevation. They are assumed to be assembly marks, provided by the masons who carved the stones to guide those involved in the assembly of the windows on site [Fig.31]. This is a rare, rather personal, trace of the human hand at work 650 years

Fig.31: Assembly mark on tracery interface

ago. Four inverted **Y-shaped** elements have also been recovered along with three small **X-shaped** elements. Taken together it appears that a substantial part of one of the gable windows has been recovered, though formal reassembly is inhibited by the lack of sufficient intact interfaces.

In his *Outline of European Architecture* published in 1943, Nikolaus Pevsner referred to the architecture of the Decorated period as '... the most forward, the most important, and the most inspired in Europe'. This importance was recognized in the mid-19th century and Dobson, having effected temporary repairs after the 1828 disaster, hoped that the chapels would be properly restored. In the event this did not happen. As part of the early 20th-century restoration of the Abbey, consideration was again given to the restoration of the chapels. Indeed, Temple Moore produced a proposal to rebuild them[12] in a style similar to that used for the reconstruction of the nave. Meeting with strong local opposition this idea was abandoned[13] and the chapels remained no more than a distant memory. Although not a restoration, the recovery of parts of the chapels' Decorated windows in the early 21st century does restore to the Abbey an important phase in its architectural and liturgical history.

---

[12] See Fig.8 on page 1.
[13] Jennings, 2001 pp.52–62.

6. Concerning the Service of the Church —
Evidence in the Abbey's Collections for Changes in
Access and Worship

Hugh Dixon

The removal of the north door to the Abbey in 1869 must have been
a shock to the congregation. It had been their principal entrance for
at least three centuries and probably much longer. To what extent
the nave was rebuilt before and after the Scottish destructions
around 1300 is not known, and whether there was more than a
ruinous nave by the time the Priory was dissolved in 1537 is still
debated. The west door, it seems, had been long abandoned. And
because the southern access to the church was reserved largely for
Canons and others living in the claustral buildings, the usual
entrance for local people would have been from the north. This
situation was reinforced after the Dissolution when the Priory and
all the grounds to the south and west became private. So, at the
moment when the church became the parish church, it could only be
approached from the north.[1] The most dramatic confirmation of this
came in the 17th century when the north doorway was built, or
probably rebuilt, in an elaborate classical style [Fig.32].[2] This main
entrance to the church was funded by the Mercers Company of
London which, through the will of Richard Fishborne in 1625, had

Fig.32: View of the Abbey from the north

---

[1] Wood, 1826: his map shows how the church had to be approached from
the Abbey Flags to its north, until the opening of Beaumont Street.

endowed Hexham with a second priest, called the Lecturer, to distinguish him from the priest appointed by the Lord of the Manor.

The doorway was very large with double doors ten feet high and an elaborate entablature and curved pediment reaching up another five feet to the lower edge of the North Transept's great lancet windows. Flanking the doors, set against piers with channelled rustication, were fluted Roman Doric pilasters with bases and capitals. The entablature included metopes, decorative panels carved with heraldic achievements, and emblems including the Mercers' Maiden.

There were many practical reasons for closing the door. It was draughty and even an internal porch had not been successful on stormy days. Direct access to the graveyard was no longer an advantage after it closed for inhumations and was replaced by the new St Andrew's cemetery on the west road in 1859. The opening of Beaumont Street in 1866 gave better access to the church from the South Transept. Worse, the doorway's classical style was seen as intrusive, even as pagan. Not a stone of the Mercers' doorway remains in place; but we know about it from fragments of evidence

Fig.33: Photograph of Abbey from NNW before 1869
when the Mercers Doorway was removed

———(cont.)———
[2] after Hutchinson, 1776.

48

in the Abbey's possession: old prints,[3,4] one early photograph [Fig.33],[5] an engraved box lid,[6] and even a few remaining carved stones[7] from the doorway itself. In particular there is a reconstruction picture 'drawn from fragments remaining and photographs' [Fig.34][8] by Charles Clement Hodges, who for over forty years was the Abbey's resident architect, antiquarian and historian.

In a similar way, by piecing together elements of evidence, it is possible to see how changes in access and in ways of worship affected the placing and style of furnishings over recent centuries. While the evidence of the building fabric is fundamental to this understanding, the progress of compiling an inventory has shown how the Abbey's contents can be revealing. Early views, plans, records, furniture, textiles, glass, and metalwork can all play a part.

Three of the most important elements of worship deserve attention: the Celebration of Communion, preaching, and Holy Baptism. In each case, changes in emphasis in worship, as well as practical considerations, have resulted in changes in location, elevation, and furnishing. In each case, too, the rebuilding of the nave in 1907–8 demanded change.

Celebration of Communion

Canon Law, honed by custom and practice over centuries, includes instructions about church furnishings. For the Holy Table it includes an instruction that 'a convenient and decent table shall be provided

---

[3] Dugdale, 1655, in which Stephen Anderton's *North Prospect of Ye Conventual Church of Hextildenham* engraved by Daniel King [HEXAB3006] seems to show the door but in cross-hatched shadow.

[4] Hutchinson, 1776, which has an oval vignette by John Bailey showing the Abbey from the north with the Mercers Door.

[5] Hodges, 1888, Plate 2: pen-and-ink drawing of the Abbey from NNW dated 1886 shows the Mercers' Door which had been destroyed 17 years earlier 'from a photograph taken by J. P. Gibson *c.*1858' [National Monuments Record, Swindon. Neg. No. BB95/40495].

[6] HEXAB2048: A box and lid of turned oak with a medal set into the top with a view of the Abbey from NW showing the eastern chapels and the Mercers' Door; engraved 'E. Pruddah 1842'.

[7] A few pieces remain in a pile outside the NW corner of the Abbey, including parts of the cornice with its projections above the pilasters, and guttae on the underside.

[8] The left hand metope (decorative panel) in the entablature shows the Mercers Maiden. Undated 1880s. [HEXAB3029].

Fig.34: Mercers (Old North) Door; removed 1869

of wood or stone or other suitable material ... and shall stand in the main body of the church or in the chancel'.[9] At Hexham the Holy Table was placed for centuries on the main axis at the east wall. In his controversial rebuilding of the east wall, John Dobson designed the wall arcading to leave a space for the Holy Table; this can still be seen in the Vestry. When the chancel was re-ordered[10] around 1900, a larger Holy Table[11] was placed at the top of seven steps and against a rood screen[12] far enough away from the east wall to allow space for a vestry. One result is that Dobson's Holy Table[13]

---

[9] CofE, 2016, section F2 'Of the holy table'.
[10] Hodges, 1913, fold-out Plan A opp. p.8.
[11] HEXAB207.
[12] HEXAB209.
[13] HEXAB184.

is no longer in the recess made for it but in St. Etheldreda's Chapel. In the later 20th century, with more centralized, communal, Celebration of Holy Communion and the celebrant able to face the congregation, the round Holy Table[14] is brought into the Crossing where it can be more easily seen from the nave and the transepts.

Preaching

The gothic revival enthusiasm which saw the destruction of the Mercers Doorway was also the cause of many changes inside the church. Nicholson's view of the choir drawn in 1813 [Fig.35][15] shows the Georgian interior still intact with box pews, galleries, and a classical reredos at the east wall. Under the influence of preaching churches, the pulpit achieved prominence and sometimes even subordinated the Holy Table. The view shows a triple-decker pulpit — lower for leading service and prayers, middle for reading from the Bible, and the top, with sounding-board canopy, for preaching the Word. All this has vanished but this valuable image shows what

Fig.35: Nicholson's view of the choir drawn in 1813

---

[14] HEXAB163, part of the suite installed 1992.
[15] Engraved by Byrne, published 1815 and also in the last edition of Monasticon Anglicanum, 1830; reproduced by Hodges, 1888, Plate 7.

it was like. With the rebuilding of the nave a new pulpit[16] was placed at the crossing though sermons are often preached from the south-east corner of the nave.

Baptism

The Font, like the Abbey itself, is an assembly of parts from different eras. The ancient bowl, a great drum of dressed stone, may have Roman origins and could be that used in Wilfrid's church. It stands on a pedestal of alternating attached colonnettes and panels of 'dog-tooth' decoration. This occurs elsewhere in the Abbey and is typical of Early English gothic carving around 1200. The cover[17] is like a crown spire with six curling Baroque arms supporting a central finial. It is said to date from a refurbishment of about 1725[18] but could be earlier. Not least is the great spire canopy[19] which Hodges found in fragments and had restored with help from M. Ceulmans[20] a Belgian refugee during the Great War who did the carving, and Messrs Hedley who completed the construction. Hodges' design for the restoration, a fully rendered watercolour drawing of 1915, is among the Abbey's minor treasures.[21]

Of the font and its placing Canon Law[22] instructs:—

1. In every church and chapel where baptism is to be administered, there shall be provided a decent font with a cover for the keeping clean thereof.

2. The font shall stand as near to the principal entrance as conveniently may be ... and shall be set in as spacious and well-ordered surroundings as possible.

In Wilfrid's church the principal entrance was at the west end and it is likely that the font was placed near the entrance and remained in this area until the destruction of the nave. After that the font started on its travels.

---

[16] HEXAB134: designed by Temple Moore to face his new nave; dedicated 1911 [Parish Magazine Oct 1911. Colin Dallison chronology]; illustrated in Gibson photograph in Hodges, 1913, Plate V.

[17] HEXAB102.

[18] Hodges, 1888, p.45.

[19] HEXAB103.

[20] Hodges & Gibson, 1919, p.63.

[21] HEXAB3051: 'Hexham Abbey, Restoration of the Ancient Tabernacle Font Cover, Charles C. Hodges, Architect, Newcastle upon Tyne, September 29th 1915'.

[22] CofE, 2016, section F1 'Of the font'.

The London architect-antiquarian, John Carter, drew a plan of the Abbey (the earliest to survive) in 1795.[23] He shows the font in the NW corner of the choir in the angle between the north and west seats. At that time this location would have been regarded as the principle entrance to the church.

Georgian views[24] show that the transepts were largely unfurnished and seem to have been used as a narthex, or great porch, for the church [Fig.36].[25] The story then becomes more complicated. In 1853 Joseph Fairless reported,[26] as if this had happened recently, 'the ancient font has been removed from the choir and now stands in the side aisle of the south transept.' By contrast, Hodges in drawing a plan of the church as it appeared before 1858,[27] showed the font without comment in the south chapel of the North Transept (now the War Memorial Chapel). This would have made sense at that time because the North Door was still the main entrance; so parishioners would have passed it both entering and leaving.

The opening of Beaumont Street in 1866, improved access to the church from the town centre. Soon after, in 1870, the font was moved again, this time to the new vestry annexe just to the west of the Crossing [Fig.37].[28] Again, this could have been seen as 'near

---

[23] British Museum: Additional Manuscripts 29.943 folio 170. Also see Hodges, 1888 Plate 8. Hodges became aware of Carter's drawings when the illustrations of his 1888 monograph were largely prepared but nevertheless he was able to include his own facsimile copy of Carter's plan on Plate 8; and did so again in Savage & Hodges, 1907, Plate V.

[24] Graham, 1984, p.11 shows a view northward from the South Transept with no furniture except low benches at the foot of the Smithson Screen on each side of the central door. Dated 1810 yet it does not show the Mercers Door; and has no other reference.

[25] Thomas Allom 'Hexham Church, Northumberland' engraved by J. Sands. Published by Fisher Son & Co. London 1833; this view southwards from the North transept shows one bench, a coffin on trestles and a pulpit on the west side of the Crossing. The latter may be an exaggerated version of the mediaeval pulpitum which was stored here before being moved to the chancel, or it could be the triple-decker moved from the chancel about this time.

[26] Fairless, 1853, p.7.

[27] Hodges, 1888, Plate 8. In his Preface, Hodges acknowledged Mr R. J Johnston, architect of Newcastle 'for the loan of his drawings of the church, which were made before the destruction of 1858'. These drawings, no doubt returned to their owner, have yet to be located.

[28] Northumberland Archives: Gibson photograph NRO1876/F/3076.

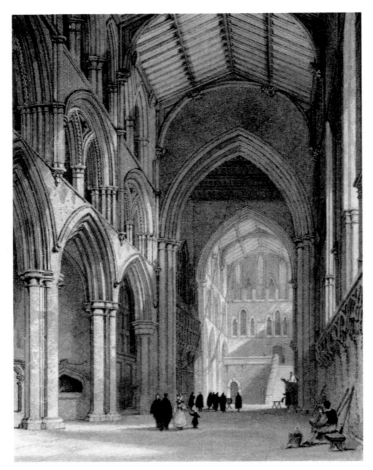

Fig.36: Transepts looking south 1833 by Thomas Allom

the principal entrance' and the arrangement seems to have worked for a generation. About 1907, when the vestry was removed to make way for the new nave, the font was moved to the south chapel of the South Transept (now St Etheldreda's Chapel). Reading desks were placed on three sides and a sort of baptistery formed. A view of about this time [Fig.38] shows that Roman altars were stored close to the south wall; the whole arrangement looks very cramped. This was seen, presumably, as a temporary measure and the font was still appropriately close to the new principal entrance through the Slype in the South Transept.

Fig.37: Font on west side of crossing

With the building of the nave in 1907–08 came the opportunity to move the font yet again. The architect, Temple Moore, as keen an ecclesiologist as Hodges, wanted to place the font near the entrance door. But which was the principal entrance? The west door had been restored. The south-west doorway to the cloister (and to Beaumont St) was likely to be popular for those coming from the town centre. And still there lingered, it seems, a wish to return to the north side. A new door was formed in the North Nave Aisle with access from the Abbey Flags. Temple Moore's plan for the new nave shows the font set on the west side of the most westerly pier between the nave and aisle (in what is now the Children's Corner).[29] Although a faculty was given for this move, it does not

---

[29] Savage & Hodges, 1907, Plate XXVIII.

Fig.38: Font in south transept chapel [CND postcard]

seem to have happened. Funds were needed.[30] Minds changed. There was a difficult change in level needing more steps inside the church leaving less room for the font.

There was also a clear wish to give the font prominence, to raise it on not two but three steps and to make these octagonal, a traditional shape for fonts. There was also a strong tradition that the font was of such importance that, where possible, it should be placed on the main axis of the church — so that worshippers had literally to pass around it on entering and leaving. Finally, through the efforts of Hodges, the medieval canopy was restored and it was of such a height that it would have been awkward to suspend it beneath the aisle arcade. So the dramatic change was made and the font was given its present position 'as near to the principal entrance as conveniently may be' and 'set in as spacious and well-ordered surroundings as possible.'

The Rector, Canon E Sydney Savage, must have been a strong influence here as, no doubt, he was in the whole reordering of the church. To mark the return of the font to the west end of the church

---

[30] Savage & Hodges, 1907, p.viii lists among proposed works totalling almost £10,000, a modest £150 for the font.

there was a presentation of a great ewer,[31] flask-shaped, of silver-plated copper, with engraved arms, and neck and waist bands decorated with enamels and polished stone 'jewels' [Fig.39]. It bears the Canon's initials and date (1916): 'ESS MCMXVI'. For many years it was shown on the steps of the font.[32] It is not hard to imagine the Canon wielding this triumph of revived medieval craftsmanship, at the font, one of the Abbey's most successful conservation projects, and in the new Nave, one of the last great monuments of the English gothic revival.

Fig.39: Ewer on steps of Font

---

[31] HEXAB2080.
[32] e.g. Taylor, 1965, p.24.

Tailpiece

It is almost a century and a half since the doorway in the North transept was blocked. Access is still a matter of preference and debate, though there are no current proposals for blocking doors. A great debt is owed to Charles Hodges for gathering and recording early evidences for the Abbey. In our time, Colin Dallison's exemplary stewardship of records has been fundamental to building both the inventory and understanding of the Abbey. This paper could not have been written without his help, as well as that of fellow inventory volunteers and members of the Conservation Advisory Panel.

7. A Seemly and Good Order:
Hexham Abbey's Collection of Prayer Books

Chris Simmons

From 1549 onwards, with the passing of the various Acts for Uniformity of Common Prayer, the Book of Common Prayer (BCP) and the Bible in English were the principal working tools of any Church of England minister. The BCP provided the only unconditionally permissible forms of public liturgy. Arguably this is still true, as more recently authorized forms generally require some form of agreement between minister and people before they can be used, even if that agreement may amount to little more than silent acquiescence. There exists a great deal of published information about the BCP's history, theology and language.[1] This essay does not attempt to treat such broad topics, but is confined to a brief survey of four copies in Hexham Abbey's collection.

1796

The oldest copies[2] date from 1796. They form an identical pair, printed by John Burges, Printer to Cambridge University Press 1793–1802. It is possible that they were used by the Rector and the Lecturer, or possibly by the Rector and the Parish Clerk. One shows slightly more wear to the spine and binding than the other.

The most curious feature of these books is that although the contents page lists the entire standard contents of the BCP, a great deal is in fact missing [Fig.40]. Omitted are all the texts that would normally be found between the *Prayers and Thanksgivings upon several occasions* and *The Psalter or Psalms of David.*[3] In practice, therefore, these copies can have been used only at Morning and Evening Prayer, although rather unexpectedly they do include the Forms of Prayer to be used at Sea and the Ordering of Bishops, Priests and Deacons, none of which would have had frequent use in the Abbey.

---

[1] e.g. Hefling and Shattuck (eds), 2006.

[2] HEXAB5505.1 & .2.

[3] Omitted are: the Collects, Epistles and Gospels for Sundays and Holy Days throughout the year; the Catechism; the Services of Holy Communion, Public Baptism, Private Baptism, Adult Baptism, Confirmation, Matrimony, Visitation of the Sick, Communion of the Sick, Burial, Thanksgiving after Childbirth; the Commination of Sinners.

THE

CONTENTS OF THIS BOOK.

AN *Act for the Uniformity of Common Prayer and Service of the Church, and Administration of the Sacraments.*
An Act for the Uniformity of Publick Prayers, and Administration of Sacraments, and other Rites and Ceremonies: And for establishing the Form of Making, Ordaining, and Consecrating Bishops, Priests and Deacons, in the Church of England.
The Preface.
Concerning the Service of the Church.
Concerning Ceremonies, why some be abolished, and some retained.
The Order how the Psalter is appointed to be read.
The Order how the rest of the holy Scripture is appointed to be read.
Tables of Proper Lessons for the Sundays and Holy-Days throughout the Year.
A Table of Proper Psalms on certain Days.
The Calendar, with the Table of Lessons.
Tables and Rules for the Feasts and Fasts through the whole Year.
The Order for Morning Prayer.
The Order for Evening Prayer.
The Creed of Saint Athanasius.
The Litany.
Prayers and Thanksgivings upon several occasions.
The Collects, Epistles, and Gospels, to be used at the Ministration of the holy Communion, throughout the Year.
The Order for the Ministration of the holy Communion.
The Ministration of Publick Baptism of Infants, to be used in the Church.
The Ministration of Private Baptism of Children in Houses.
The Ministration of Baptism to such as are of riper Years, and able to answer for themselves.
The Catechism.
The Order of Confirmation.
The Form of Solemnization of Matrimony.
The Order for the Visitation of the Sick.
The Communion of the Sick.
The Order for the Burial of the Dead.
The Thanksgiving of Women after Child-bearing.
A Commination, or Denouncing of God's Anger and Judgements against Sinners.
The Psalter or Psalms of David.
Forms of Prayer to be used at Sea.
The Form or Manner of Making, Ordaining, and Consecrating of Bishops, Priests, and Deacons.
A Form of Prayer for the 5th Day of November, being the Day kept in Memory of the Papists' Conspiracy.
A Form of Prayer for the 30th Day of January, being the Day kept in Memory of the Martyrdom of King Charles the First.
A Form of Prayer for the 29th Day of May, being the Day kept in Memory of the Birth and Return of King Charles the Second.
A Form of Prayer for the 25th Day of October, being the Day on which his Majesty began his happy Reign.
Articles of Religion.

Fig.40: Book of Common Prayer 1796 – Contents page

Their particular interest lies in the appendix, technically not part of the BCP, which consists of Tate and Brady's metrical versions of the Psalms [Fig.41], prefaced by the Order in Council of King Charles II dated 3rd December 1696 permitting their use *"in all such Churches, Chapels and Congregations, as shall think fit to receive the same"*, and the following commendation by The Rt Revd Henry Compton (Bishop of London 1676–1714) for their use in his diocese — an early instance of episcopal, and an unusual instance of royal, enthusiasm for an authorized alternative!

May 23d, 1698. HIS Majesty having Allowed, and Permitted the Use of a New Version of the Psalms of David, by Dr. Brady, and Mr. Tate, in all Churches, Chapels and Congregations; I cannot do less than wish a good Success to this Royal Indulgence: For I find it a Work done with so much Judgment and Ingenuity, that I am persuaded, it may take off that unhappy Objection, which has hitherto lain against the Singing Psalms; and dispose that part of Divine Service to much more Devotion. And I do heartily recommend the Use of this Version to all my Brethren within my Diocese. H. LONDON.

The necessity for a Royal Warrant to authorize any deviation from the original contents of the BCP is a reminder that while its spiritual authority derives from Cranmer's genius as a liturgist and linguist, its legal authority is entirely the creation of the political establishment of the Church of England under the Crown in Parliament. The twists and turns of English history between 1547 and, say, 1745 made it a kind of totem of loyalty to the state and the Protestant *status quo* which certainly persisted well into the reign of

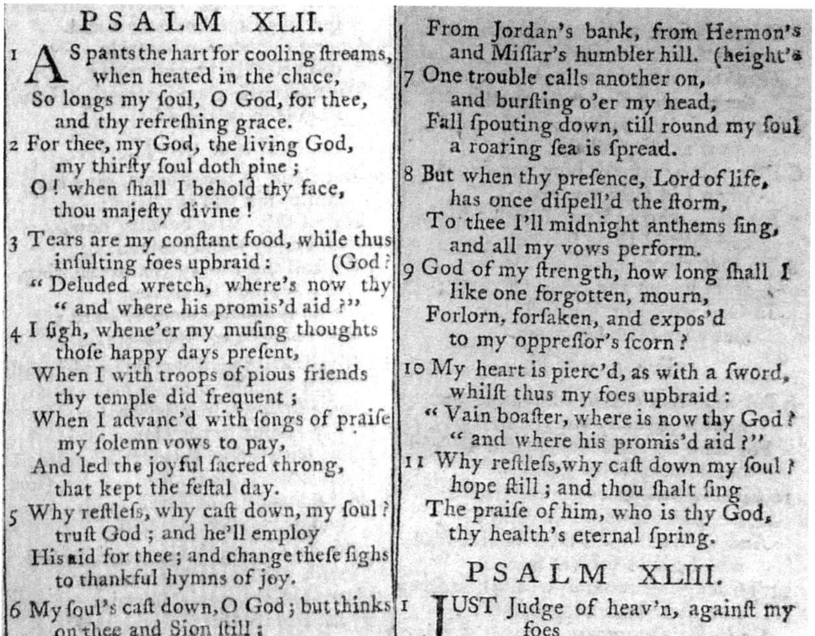

PSALM XLII.

1 AS pants the hart for cooling streams,
when heated in the chace,
So longs my soul, O God, for thee,
and thy refreshing grace.
2 For thee, my God, the living God,
my thirsty soul doth pine;
O! when shall I behold thy face,
thou majesty divine!
3 Tears are my constant food, while thus
insulting foes upbraid: (God?
" Deluded wretch, where's now thy
" and where his promis'd aid?"
4 I sigh, whene'er my musing thoughts
those happy days present,
When I with troops of pious friends
thy temple did frequent;
When I advanc'd with songs of praise
my solemn vows to pay,
And led the joyful sacred throng,
that kept the festal day.
5 Why restless, why cast down, my soul?
trust God; and he'll employ
His aid for thee; and change these sighs
to thankful hymns of joy.
6 My soul's cast down, O God; but thinks
on thee and Sion still;

From Jordan's bank, from Hermon's
and Mizar's humbler hill. (height's
7 One trouble calls another on,
and bursting o'er my head,
Fall spouting down, till round my soul
a roaring sea is spread.
8 But when thy presence, Lord of life,
has once dispell'd the storm,
To thee I'll midnight anthems sing,
and all my vows perform.
9 God of my strength, how long shall I
like one forgotten, mourn,
Forlorn, forsaken, and expos'd
to my oppressor's scorn?
10 My heart is pierc'd, as with a sword,
whilst thus my foes upbraid:
" Vain boaster, where is now thy God?
" and where his promis'd aid?"
11 Why restless, why cast down my soul?
hope still; and thou shalt sing
The praise of him, who is thy God,
thy health's eternal spring.

PSALM XLIII.

1 JUST Judge of heav'n, against my
foes

Fig.41: 1796 Metrical Psalms of Tate and Brady.
NB: Psalm XLII still in current use

Queen Victoria, and had not disappeared even as late as 1928, when a very conservative attempt to alter it in certain details failed, because of a supposed Romanizing tendency, to receive the necessary parliamentary approval. Thus the need to replace individual copies arose only infrequently, when the old one was too worn either for repair or further use, or when one of the very limited permitted changes actually occurred.

The most obvious of these occasions for change was the accession of a new sovereign. Not only would the names mentioned in the state prayers need alteration, but a revised service to mark the anniversary of the accession of the new monarch would have to be authorized, again by Royal Warrant. This, in fact, was the most common method of making changes. Parliamentary legislation was generally not required until the latter part of Queen Victoria's reign, by which time it was very evidently needed to regularize changes in liturgical practice that were already commonplace, though still strictly illegal.[4]

1831

King William IV succeeded to the throne in 1830, following the death of his brother King George IV. This may explain the Abbey's acquisition of the huge volume[5] with the cover inscription 'HEXHAM CHURCH 1831'. The title page describes this book as containing the Rites and Ceremonies of the United Church of England and Ireland. The two churches were united into "one Protestant Episcopal church", as a consequence of the Act of Union of 1801. The Irish Church Act 1869 separated the Irish part of the church again and disestablished it, the Act coming into effect on 1 January 1871.

As well as all the usual BCP contents this copy contains [Fig.42] the complete Constitutions and Canons Ecclesiastical as they had been drawn up and agreed by the Convocation of the Province of Canterbury in 1603, under the authority of King James I. With one exception these Canons have all been repealed and replaced.[6]

---

[4] e.g. The Act of Uniformity Amendment Act 1872 ('The Shortened Services Act') which permitted the omission of the opening sections of Morning and Evening Prayer in certain circumstances.

[5] HEXAB5503.

[6] Specifically unrepealed to this day is the following part of Canon 113 of 1603, relating to the secrecy of the confessional:
Provided always, that if any man confess his secret and hidden sins to the

(cont.)

19. *Loiterers not to be suffered near the Church in time of Divine Service.*

THE Church-wardens or Quest-men, and their assistants, shall not suffer any idle persons to abide either in the Church-yard, or Church-porch, during the time of Divine Service, or Preaching; but shall cause them either to come in, or to depart.

Fig.42: Canon 19:— of the duties of churchwardens

This book contains the Accession Service for King William IV, to be used on 26th June each year. The contents page, however, mistakenly continues to refer to the service for 29th January, the accession date of his predecessor.

Queen Victoria succeeded her uncle William in 1837. The early part of her reign saw profound changes in English society, expressed in religious terms through the flourishing of the Oxford Movement, and the continuing process of catholic emancipation following the Roman Catholic Relief Act of 1829 which, among other things, permitted Roman Catholics to sit in the House of Commons. The links between loyal citizenship and religious conformity were loosening, but the BCP still contained several "state" services (in addition to that for the anniversary of monarch's accession) which were markedly anti-Catholic in their origin and content. These commemorated the Gunpowder Plot, the beheading of King Charles I, the restoration of King Charles II and the arrival of the protestant King William III after the deposition of the Catholic King James II [Fig.43]. All are contained in the Abbey BCP of 1831. By 1859 they were no longer socially or politically tolerable, and a Royal Warrant was issued commanding their discontinuance and omission from future printings of the BCP.

————(cont.)————————

minister, for the unburdening of his conscience, and to receive spiritual consolation and ease of mind from him; we do not in any way bind the said minister by this our Constitution, but do straitly charge and admonish him, that he do not at any time reveal and make known to any person whatsoever any crime or offence so committed to his trust and secrecy (except they be such crimes as by the laws of this realm his own life may be called into question for concealing the same), under pain of irregularity.

A FORM OF

PRAYER WITH THANKSGIVING,

To be ufed yearly upon the Fifth Day of *November*, for the happy Deliverance of King *JAMES* I. and the three Eftates of *England*, from the moft traiterous and bloody-intended Maffacre by Gunpowder: And alfo for the happy Arrival of His Majefty King *William* on this Day, for the Deliverance of our Church and Nation.

¶ *The Minister of every Parish shall give warning to his Parishioners publickly in the Church at Morning Prayer, the Sunday before, for the due Observation of the said Day. And after Morning Prayer, or Preaching, upon the said Fifth Day of November, shall read publickly, distinctly, and plainly, the Act of Parliament, made in the third Year of King James the First, for the Observation of it.*

Fig.43: Form of Service for 5th November, Heading and Rubric

1862

This change may explain the presentation to the Abbey of a new BCP[7] in 1862. The plate inside the front cover records that it was presented by The Revd Henry Christopher Barker MA, Lecturer. As massive as the copy it replaced, it presumably rested on a suitably massive reading desk which, before the restoration of the nave in the early 20th century, would have stood in the candle-lit gloom of the Abbey quire. It contains the full text of the Royal Warrant of 1859 referred to above.

Equally interesting in terms of Victorian social history are the loose-leaf documents preserved between the pages containing the Collects, Epistles, and Gospels for the 12th and 13th Sundays after Trinity:

> *To the Incumbents of the Diocese of Newcastle.*
>
> *Benwell Tower, Newcastle-upon-Tyne*
>
> *January 6th, 1898*
>
> *Reverend and dear Brother, Let me commend to your careful consideration the subjoined letter from the two Archbishops which reached me too late for publication in the January number of the Diocesan Gazette.*
>
> *I am, Very faithfully yours,*
>
> *EDGAR NEWCASTLE*[8]

---

[7] HEXAB5502.
[8] Edgar Jacob, second Bishop of Newcastle 1896–1903.

To the Clergy of the Provinces of Canterbury and York.

REVEREND AND DEAR BRETHREN,

It is impossible for any Christian in this country not to watch with the deepest concern the dispute which for some time past has stopped the work of the engineering trades. Both sides sustain very heavy losses, and the money so wasted can never be replaced. And all such conflicts are attended by the serious danger of driving much of the business out of the country, very possibly never to return. And, if this were to happen, the widespread distress, and even destitution, which must inevitably follow it, would be very difficult to estimate.

To judge justly between the two sides is possible only for those who know the detailed working of the whole trade. It may be that with many of us natural sympathy would be drawn more strongly towards those whose very means of existence are in peril. But sympathy cannot determine a question of justice.

But if we cannot judge, and therefore cannot take one side against the other, yet we can do all that within us lies to promote that spirit of human brotherhood and mutual loving kindness which alone can rob such conflicts of their bitterness, and lead men to treat one another in a temper of conciliation. We can urge on both sides to make peace and goodwill the primary aim of all negotiation, to strive for equity and not for victory, to endeavour each to put himself in the other's place and to see with the other's eyes, and look for a settlement in which mutual goodwill hereafter shall rest on a sense of mutual fair treatment at the present time.

And, above all, we can pray for such a result; we can pray that God's Holy Spirit may give to all, and especially to those who are disputing, light to see what is just and equitable between man and man, lovingkindness to follow it, whether in dealing with those who are richer or those who are poorer, mutual trust and confidence in all relations of business.

To this we beseech you, brethren, to exhort your people, and for this purpose we recommend the following prayer to be said in all churches in both our provinces :—

"Almighty God, the Source of all Justice and the Giver of all Peace, by Whose Providence all human occupations are ordained for the comfort of the sons of men, and to Whom all men are responsible for their conduct therein, we beseech Thee to look with pity on the dispute which is now causing great distress to many of our people and bringing into peril their means of employment and subsistence. Give to all the spirit of brotherly lovingkindness, of mutual trust, of equitable consideration, and so bring them to stable peace and harmony, that they may henceforth fulfil their service of mankind to Thy honour and glory, through Jesus Christ our Lord. Amen."

We commend you, brethren, to the love of God in the name of our Lord Jesus Christ.

F. CANTUAR.
W. EBOR.

Fig.44: Archbishops' pastoral letter of 1898

There follows a letter [Fig.44] from the Archbishops of York and Canterbury to all the clergy, referring to *"the dispute which for some time past has stopped the work of the engineering trade."* The letter points out the damaging consequences of the dispute, the difficulty of judging between the two sides involved, and the necessity of working and praying for a peaceful and just outcome. It contains a prayer recommended by the Archbishops for use in all churches of both provinces, and is signed: F. Cantuar and W. Ebor.[9]

The dispute referred to originated in Barrow-in-Furness and would no doubt have had a major effect on the heavy industry located in Newcastle diocese:

The lock-out and strike in the British engineering industry, which took place between July 1897 and January 1898, was one of the most bitter and protracted labour disputes of the 1890s. As "the first major national strike or lock-out in British history", a dispute set against the turbulent background of "new unionism" and socialist influences within the 91,500-strong Amalgamated Society of Engineers, and fought over the issues of working hours, the rights of employers in their own "shops" and the vexed question of the introduction of technical improvements into

---

[9] Frederick Temple, Archbishop of Canterbury 1896–1902, and William Maclagan, Archbishop of York 1891–1908.

the industry, the conflict had great political and economic significance.[10]

1936

This copy[11] was inscribed on November 11th 1936 by The Revd J.V.C. Farquhar, Rector of Hexham: *In grateful memory of Hannah Benson Woodman, a loved and loving Mother and a Friend to all good causes.*[Fig.45] She had died on 29th January 1935. To judge

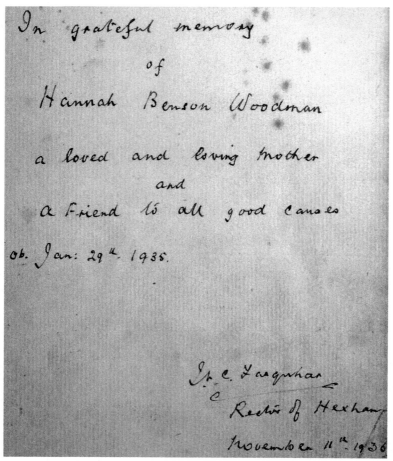

Fig.45: Dedicatory inscription

---

[10] Todd, 1975, p.33.
[11] HEXAB5514.

from the condition of the pages it was used for a number of years, particularly at Evening Prayer. This book contains the only service in the entire history of the BCP which can never have been used: the Form of Prayer and Service authorized by King Edward VIII to be used yearly on 20th January to mark the anniversary of his accession [Fig.46]. Only five days after Canon Farquhar wrote his inscription the King informed the Prime Minister, Stanley Baldwin, of his desire to marry Mrs Simpson. The abdication crisis unfolded very rapidly, and Edward ceased to be King on 11th December, after less than a year on the throne.

The custom of marking the anniversary of the reigning monarch's accession began during the reign of Queen Elizabeth I. Her tenth anniversary, on 17th November 1568, was marked with the ringing of bells. The date became known as "Queene's Day". As her reign progressed, it was celebrated with increased fervour and, long after her death, it continued to be observed as a day of Protestant rejoicing and expression of anti-Catholic feeling.

On the accession of King James VI of Scotland as James I of England a form of prayer and thanksgiving was issued for use in all churches "upon his entry to this kingdom". The execution of King Charles I and establishment of the Commonwealth in 1649 naturally

"EDWARD R.I.

"WHEREAS by a Royal Warrant of His late Majesty King George the Fifth dated the Eighth day of December, One thousand nine hundred "and twenty-five, certain Forms of Prayer and Service were made for the "Sixth day of May and commanded to be printed and published and "annexed to the Book of Common Prayer and Liturgy of the Church of "England to be used yearly in all Churches and Chapels within the "Provinces of Canterbury and York:

"NOW Our Will and Pleasure is that the said Royal Warrant be "revoked, and that the use of the said Forms of Prayer and Service be "discontinued; and that the Forms of Prayer and Service hereunto annexed "be forthwith printed and published and annexed to the Book of Common "Prayer and Liturgy of the Church of England to be used yearly on the "Twentieth day of January in all Churches and Chapels within the "Provinces of Canterbury and York.

"GIVEN at Our Court at Saint James's, the Seventeenth day of "February, 1936; In the First Year of Our Reign.

"By His Majesty's Command.

"JOHN SIMON."

Fig.46: Royal warrant for the accession service of
King Edward VIII

put an end to the observance. A different form of service was authorized to celebrate the restoration of King Charles II on 29th May 1660. In 1685 King James II ordered the preparation of a special form of prayer and thanksgiving for the anniversary of his accession and a revised version of the old service was prepared. After falling out of use during the reign of King William III and Queen Mary II, the service was revised and used again during the reign of Queen Anne and (with appropriate further amendments) all subsequent monarchs.

The present Queen's accession day is 6th February, and all present printings of the Book of Common Prayer include the Royal Warrant dated 26th July 1958 and the current forms of service for the day.

8. Abbey Vestments

Neel Lever and Christine Seal

Church vestments today have evolved from the everyday clothing of the Roman Empire. Symbolism has played an important part in our lives since the world began, with our use of symbols covering all aspects of life, death, and immortality. Artists, craftsmen, and designers have long used symbols to convey messages and meanings.[1] For example, the Holy Spirit can be represented in two ways: as a dove often seen descending and haloed, or as fire where seven or nine or 12 tongues of flame are displayed. Fire is a reference to the Pentecost.[2]

Liturgical colours only became regularised in the 13th century and carry their own symbolism. Colour in the church identifies blue for the Virgin Mary; it is the colour of sky and represents heavenly love. Green is the colour of life and of the triumph of life over death, and red, the colour of passions and the fire of Pentecost.[3] Purple is a royal colour and can represent pomp and pride, but is overwhelmingly seen as the colour of penitence and humility, especially in Lent. White and gold can show radiance and glory, and represent the sun and divine power.[4] Among these colours green has a peculiar history and is not strictly an Anglican colour although it was used in England at an early date. At first it seems to have had only a monastic use. It was seen in abbeys but not for some time in cathedrals or parish churches. It was used for processional copes but not for chasubles, stoles, or altar hangings until a later date.[5]

The choice of these symbolically-charged liturgical colours is also controlled by the church's seasons. White is used for marriage and baptism, and for all great festivals, except Whitsuntide and feast-days of martyred saints when red is used. Red is also used during Holy Week, except at Holy Communion on Maundy Thursday. Purple or violet is used for Advent and in Lent from Ash Wednesday until the day before Palm Sunday. Green is used from the day after the Presentation until Shrove Tuesday, and from the day after Pentecost until the eve of All Saints' Day, except when other provision is made.

---

[1] Messent, 1996.
[2] Taylor, 2004, p.75.
[3] Taylor, 2004, p.23.
[4] Messent, 1996, p.39.
[5] Hall, 1913, p.44.

Vestments and their Uses[6]

A **Cope** was developed from a Roman cloak-like garment and is semi-circular, opening down the front. The word 'Cope' is derived from 'caput' meaning head.[7] The clasp, where seen, is known as a **morse** and lies below the throat. On the back, the cope retains a vestigial hood which was triangular or shield-shaped. Orphrey bands run the full length of the front opening. An *orphrey* is a form of often highly detailed embroidery, in which typically simple materials are made into complex patterns. In 1182 and 1183 Henry II of England spent lavishly on orphreys.

A **Stole** is a long strip of cloth matching the chasuble, approximately nine feet (275 cm) long, tapering from approximately two-and-a-half inches (7 cm) wide at the neck to three to four inches (8–10 cm) at the bottom. A simple cross marks the centre. The Stole is placed around the neck and often has rich decoration at the ends. It is symbolic of the yoke of Christ, the priest kissing the cross worked on the back when it is put on.

A **Chasuble** is worn only for Holy Communion. It is a seamless robe and its origins go back to an outdoor garment of Biblical times. Rather like a poncho, it is a cover with a hole in the centre for the head. Various decorations appear on the chasuble including a cross on the back (the cross Jesus carried to Calvary); a plain stripe on the front (the pillar at which he was scourged); a transverse beam of a cross, usually at an acute angle, suggests the form taken by the Lord's arms extended upon the cross; a cross on the front (the priest should diligently behold the footsteps of Christ). The Chasubles considered in this chapter all have beautiful embroidery.

The **Maniple** is placed on the left forearm and its colour, shape, and decoration echo the Stole. Various thoughts as to its origins include that it signifies 'sheaves of good work' or is the napkin Christ used to dry the disciples' feet at the Last Supper.

Chalice Veil; a square of approximately 20–24 inches (50–60 cm) with the fabric matching the priest's vestments. Decoration is usually on one side so this could be seen from the front when the chalice is covered.

The **Burse** is a square board carried above the chalice. Two boards are joined and hinged along one side to form a 'case' or 'purse'. When not in use it stands hinge side uppermost at the side

---

[6] Anon., 1962; Smelt, 1985.
[7] Taylor, 2004, p.259.

of the altar. The fabric matches the vestments and is usually lined with white linen, but not always.

Abbey Vestments

St Andrew's Cope

This cope [Fig.47][8] was bought by Canon Lemon from Faithcraft in Westminster for the Queen's visit in 1974. The cope is made in a beige and cream brocade with printed blue and gold embroidered bands. The cross is in gold fabric with a background of blue printed brocade. There is deep metallic gold fringing around the shield. The Cross of St Andrew is on the shield and is an illusion to his humility in refusing to suffer on a cross similar to that on which his Master, Christ, suffered.[9] The shield is held in place by blue fabric covered buttons.

Fig.47: St Andrew's cope rear view of shield

---

[8] HEXAB4200.
[9] Marshall, 1894, p.127.

Lamb of God Chasuble

As yet we have not established when this and associated items were obtained by the Abbey. The Lamb of God or *Agnus Dei* is depicted in the cream chasuble[Fig.48],[10] and is the image of gentleness, meekness and suffering, a symbol of Christ. The chasuble is made of Old Gold coloured material with a damask orphrey embroidered with gold and silk floss, couched and satin stitch with a central design of a lamb carrying a bannered cross. The orphrey is edged with braid. The back orphrey is plain. The whole has a lining of apricot satin. The lamb is here shown in a position of triumph with one of its legs hooked around the pole of a flag. The flag is made up of a red cross on a white background.[11] Embroidered flowers and leaves surround the lamb, also shown on the burse [Fig.49].[12]

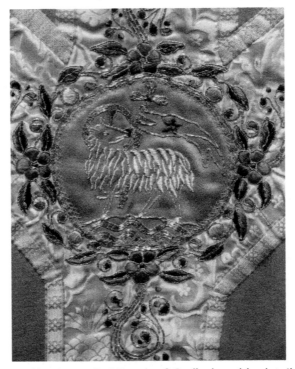

Fig.48: *Agnus Dei* (Lamb of God) chasuble detail

---

[10] HEXAB4013.
[11] Taylor, 2004, pp.70–72; Whittick, 1935, p.55.

Fig.49: *Agnus Dei* burse

Cream Chasuble

This chasuble [Fig.50][13] has a beautiful Italian quilted Celtic knot on the back set in a triangle. It is thought to have been made in 2005 as a not-too-close copy of one made in 1997 by Janet Dewey,

Fig.50: Italian quilted chasuble
detail of Celtic knot on reverse of vestment

---

[12] HEXAB4013.5.
[13] HEXAB4009

Ecclesiastical Embroiderer from Bromley, Kent. The background of this triangle is random quilted. The accessories [Fig.51] have a triquetra in Italian quilting. In Latin, **triquetra** means "three cornered". This symbol is also called the Trinity Knot or Celtic Triangle. The triquetra [Fig.52] is composed of three interlocked *vesicæ piscis*, marking the intersection of three circles. It is most commonly a symbol of the Holy Trinity (Father, Son, and Holy Spirit) used by the Celtic Christian Church, sometimes stylized as three interlaced fish. It also features the Abbeys' Frith Stool.[14]

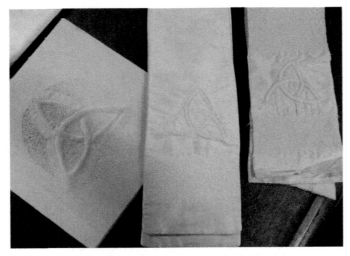

Fig.51: Burse, chalice veil, and maniple all with triquetra

Fig.52: Triquetra

Red Chasuble

This set of vestments was given in October 1984 by Mrs Dulcie Richardson[15] in memory of her late husband Canon Hugh

---

[14] HEXAB6502.
[15] Anon, 1984.

Richardson. The chasuble is made of red slub dupion and is lined with cream taffeta. On the front and back are embroidered and couched wheat ears [Fig.53].[16] The accessories also have the wheat ears embroidered on them [Fig.54].

Fig.53: Red chasuble
detail of embroidered wheat ears

Fig.54: Burse, maniple, chalice veil

[16] HEXAB4033.

The Celtic Cope

The Celtic cope is in use in the Abbey and is a beautiful vestment in gold dupion, with a green/mauve satin lining. The cope was made for its owner in 1994 to celebrate 25 years as a priest.

Celtic art found expression and grew in 'Gospel' books, stone carvings, and metal work. Interlace was one variation of the many Celtic art forms that flourished. The Lindisfarne Gospels and Northumbria were the inspiration for the cope and it includes Celtic art and its intricate interlace.[17]

The design of the cope comprises rectangular shaped Celtic knots, interspersed with a Latin cross of various colours on a coloured background [Fig.55]. Celtic knotwork consists of an over and under interlaced ribbon design. It is an 'endless' knot, having no start and finish and symbolizes love and devotion.[18] The knot appears on the bands down the front of the cope and on the collar at the neck. The five crosses are taken from each parish the owner served in. The fourth one down is for 'Christ the Carpenter' and the

Fig.55: Celtic knot and cross band

[17] Wiechec, 1980, introduction.
[18] Messent, 1993, p.36.

cross is formed on nails. The front is held together with a brass 'morse', a clasp of a Celtic animal, a Lindworm.

The back has two panels of Celtic birds worked in Italian Quilting, with the wings of the birds worked in blue needle-lace [Fig.56]. The *Chi-Rho* or letter "P" and a cross appears on the back and is one of the earliest forms of Christogram. The Chi-Rho is formed by superimposing the first two capital letters 'chi' (X) and 'rho' (P) of the Greek word "ΧΡΙΣΤΟΣ" (= Christos) in such a way as to produce a monogram. The Chi-Rho can represent either Christ or Christianity.[19]

Fig.56: Back of cope showing
Celtic birds and *chi-rho*

---

[19] www.religionfacts.com/chi-rho (5.7.2016).

The Victoria and Albert Vestments

In 1902 Alice Hedley, wife of an army surgeon, came to the Victoria and Albert Museum (V&A) with some church vestments she wished to sell. She said they came from Hexham. They consisted of three chasubles and a maniple, made between 1500 and 1525. They are all of English needlework[20] and were made for Robert Thornton, the 22nd Abbot of Jervaulx (1510–1533). The exact date of his death is unknown, but the archiepiscopal commission for the blessing of his successor, Adam Sedbergh, is dated 20th November 1533. Sometime after the dissolution of Jervaulx in 1537, its last dean, William Willes (died 1552) brought Robert Thornton's body to the church of St Mary and St Alkelda at Middleham for reburial near its pulpit.[21]

Fig.57: Red chasuble front detail

---

[20] Kendrick, 1902.

One chasuble is of crimson silk velvet, with embroidery in coloured silks and silver gilt thread and spangles, partly worked on linen and afterwards applied [Fig.57]. The repeating design consists of floral devices, arranged in radiating lines to suit the shape of a cope, from which this chasuble has been cut. On the back is a cross-shaped *orphrey* [Fig.58] containing the following figures beneath canopies: St Peter, an Old Testament figure, St Matthias, and a man holding a scroll. The left arm of the orphrey has a representation of the Head of Our Saviour (originally the morse of the cope) and the right arm is in fragments. The background of each compartment is a silver gilt thread and coloured floss silks couched in wavy and lozenge diapers. The chasuble is trimmed with yellow and green silk braid and has a reddish linen lining (now faded).[22]

Another chasuble, a black mourning vestment, is decorated with Last Judgement imagery and Thornton's rebus (the initials R.T. to the side of a crozier impaling a mitre, which rises from a barrel or tun, forming a pun on the last syllable of his name). This chasuble was recycled from a pall, a cloth used to cover a coffin. The

Fig.58: Red chasuble back orphrey

--------(cont.)--------

[21] Carter, 2013.
[22] Victoria & Albert Museum No: 695-1902.

chasuble is made of black silk velvet with orphreys of crimson silk velvet, embroidered in coloured silks, silver gilt and silver thread and spangles.[23] It is thought that the vestment survived thanks to its continued use by recusants but its shape was altered to accord with changing fashions in liturgical dress. Although this mourning chasuble is in many ways a typical example of late medieval English ecclesiastical embroidery, it is unusual in a number of respects. It is the only surviving English vestment which is decorated with images taken from contemporary depictions of the Last Judgement. Lengthy texts taken from the Cistercian liturgy appear on the vestment, suggesting that Thornton used it to assert his Cistercian identity and to display his exalted ecclesiastical and social status, but also as a visual prompt for prayers from the Jervaulx community assembling for his Requiem Mass.[24]

We cannot confirm whether the vestments in the V&A originated in Hexham, but both sides of the Hedley family were Roman Catholic. Previous owners in the 17th century would have used the vestments at great personal risk.

Conclusion

The designs on the vestments contain interesting symbolism which has a long history in the Christian church. Only a few of the vestments held in the Abbey have been discussed and there are many more that warrant further investigation and showing to the wider public.

---

[23] Victoria & Albert Museum No: 697-1902.
[24] Carter, 2010.

9. Would Wilfrid Recognize This?
3D Digital Modelling of Hexham Abbey

Louise Hampson
& Geoff Arnott, Patrick Gibbs, Anthony Masinton

The Hexham Abbey project offered The Centre for the Study of Christianity and Culture at the University of York a wonderful opportunity to recreate for visitors an impression of what the church built by St. Wilfrid in 674, and its successors, might have looked like. To do this we would need to draw on our experience of digital modelling and the body of available academic expertise. Our goal was to convert the fragmentary evidence supplied by archaeology, manuscripts, antiquarian sources, and the surviving fabric into a detailed, three-dimensional visualization of the Anglo-Saxon and later churches, offering a unique glimpse into the Abbey's past. This is the story of that endeavour.

Digital modelling, the creation of complex three-dimensional, virtual spaces which can be explored and viewed from any angle, is not new, but it is a fast-paced and expanding field now capable of producing realistic results. Driven by an expanding market for televisual and cinematic computer graphics, plus the ever-developing computer gaming industry, the technology has developed significantly in its capabilities, allowing 3D digital artists to produce buildings and landscapes with a near photo-real appearance. Whilst this has made TV and film more believable, and games more engaging and satisfying to play, historical accuracy when representing buildings and spaces has not been the primary driver. However, alongside the entertainment industry, the academic world has begun to engage with the opportunities offered by this technology to reconstruct 'lost' environments and buildings using surviving evidence and the fruits of detailed research.[1] In other words, to actually build the buildings from the sources and see what we get! The chance to employ these techniques at existing historic sites is exciting, but also challenging: how should we deal with the gaps in our knowledge, different interpretations of evidence, and the need to balance authenticity with a satisfying visitor experience? Where is the boundary between 'reasonable conjecture' and

---

[1] Ch'ng, Gaffney, Chapman, 2013.

'fantasy' and how do we convey that distinction to visitors with clarity, but without spoiling their enjoyment and engagement?

The project team at Hexham Abbey had marshalled an impressive array of evidence and expert knowledge, and of course the abbey building itself is still in existence. The 7th-century crypt of St. Wilfrid's church survives and contains a stunning array of re-used Roman stonework, most likely from nearby Corbridge, but this was associated with a much larger church above ground within some form of monastic enclosure about which much less structural detail was known.[2] There were many tantalizing snippets of information: records of wall sections found in archaeological excavations, as well as study of the standing fabric; the chance discoveries of pieces of carved stonework; the wonderfully detailed recording of the current building and crypt by Hodges;[3] descriptions of staircases, pillars and towers in Eddius Stephanus' *Life of St Wilfrid*;[4] 12th-century accounts by Ælred of Rievaulx of the destruction and rebuilding of parts of the church.[5] There were lots of bits of information, but how did they fit together? It was in many ways like doing a jigsaw with no box lid picture, and with the certain knowledge that we did not (and never would) have all the pieces. Could we rebuild Wilfrid's church or anything even close to it?

Digital modelling is an unforgiving discipline. Unlike traditional forms of illustration, there is little scope for the kind of artistic licence that allows you to quietly fade or blur uncertainties, or merely suggest the presence of details with a few strokes of the pen. The very realism which makes the results so appealing demands a relentless precision and level of detail if it is to capture any real sense of that lost world. Low-detail block models (the digital equivalent of Lego) can be built as more abstract indicators of form and orientation, a technique we utilized to represent parts of the monastic enclosure, but they are visually less appealing and can break the illusion that you are somehow catching a glimpse into the past.

Our first task was to gather all the information we could that might give us any clues as to the physical appearance of Wilfrid's church and discuss it with the team at Hexham. The archaeological

---

[2] Alexander, 2013.
[3] Savage and Hodges, 1907.
[4] Webb, 2004, p.128.
[5] Freeland, 2006, pp.89–90.

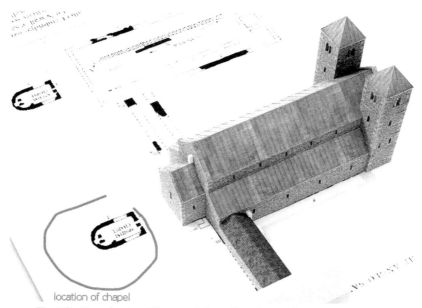

location of chapel

Fig.59: Developing the model outline from the published plan

data compiled and assessed over many years by Dr Eric Cambridge and Professor Richard Bailey amongst others was, understandably, principally concerned with the layout and development of the church and surrounding buildings from the limited amount of excavation which had been possible on such a complex site [Fig.59].[6] This provided the basis for a possible footprint for the church, but what had it looked like above ground, both inside and out? The description in Chapter 22 of Eddius Stephanus' *Life of St. Wilfrid*, written soon after Wilfrid's death in 709, appeared to give us some answers:

> *...the great depth of the foundations, the crypts of beautifully dressed stone, the vast structure supported by columns of various styles and with numerous side-aisles, the walls of remarkable height and length, the many winding passages and spiral staircases leading up and down.*

We may begin to imagine a church interior from this in our own mind, but for modelling purposes it tells us very little. How many side aisles, going from where to where? What were the 'various

---

[6] Cambridge, 2013; Bidwell, 2013; Bailey, 2013.

styles' of the columns — were they re-used Roman ones? — and how high were the walls 'of remarkable height'? Where did the 'many winding passages and spiral staircases' lead from and to? Likewise, when Ælred of Rievaulx wrote his 12th-century account of his grandfather heroically rescuing the church from a state of near collapse, with trees growing through the roof and with only a lonely shrine-keeper in attendance, it marvellously evoked the atmosphere but tells us nothing of the physical appearance of the church he found. In addition, in both cases, there are significant questions about how the writer's purpose and style affect the accuracy or historical reliability of what they wrote: sadly, they were not writing detailed descriptions for the benefit of later historians.

So beginning with the archaeological evidence we began to build a 'wireframe': a mass of 3D digital points which join up to make the bones of a building [Fig.60]. Even at this basic stage there were heated discussions about how the evidence should or could be interpreted [Fig.61]. Did the west end have two towers with some kind of porch or vestibule between them, or should the archaeological evidence be interpreted as a front with a solid screen, perhaps with smaller turrets at the top? The evidence from the ground was partial and ambiguous, so it relied in part on expert opinion and interpretation of that evidence and in part on looking for the rare surviving examples.

Fig.60: A screenshot of the detailed wireframe model of Wilfrid's church under construction

Fig.61: A close-up view of the model in progress, showing the
relationship to other buildings rendered in grey

We knew Wilfrid had travelled widely on the continent and
began his building at Hexham after he returned from Gaul (modern
France). Stone building in England had largely ceased with the end
of Roman rule, the Anglo-Saxons preferring to build in wood, so
Wilfrid would have brought styles and ideas from his travels back
to Ripon and Hexham. We looked to the continent and to
contemporary manuscripts to see if we could see what Wilfrid saw
thirteen hundred years ago. We found some details and clues and
began to build upon our basic wireframe. At this stage the model
was simply a series of blank grey blocks — uninspiring, but useful
for defining the overall proportions, layout and key features. Once
agreement on these aspects was reached, discussion turned to the
difficult questions of doors and roof lines, and of window size,
style, and position. Some elements could be extrapolated from the
evidence we did have, much had to be drawn from comparable
sources elsewhere.

The physical appearance of a model is transformed by the
application of textures, the realistic colours and surfaces which
represent different building materials, decoration or signs of wear
[Fig.62]. We know Wilfrid's church was made of stone, but did he
re-use Roman stone to build his church as he did for the crypt, or
was new stone cut by the masons he imported from Gaul? Based on
manuscript evidence we gave the church a lead roof, although this
would have been very expensive, and put some equally expensive
glass in the small windows. The question of the ancillary monastic

Look inside

Fig.62: The exterior view of Wilfrid's church as finally presented

buildings around the church was a thorny one: there was no archaeological data available and no commonly-recognized layout to copy (unlike later monastic sites), but it was agreed that it would be misleading to show the church in splendid isolation. In discussion with the project's expert advisers we compromised by populating the precinct with block buildings which remained grey, intentionally standing in strong contrast to the much more detailed model of the church and visually underlining the difference in evidential base.

The unforgiving nature of the modelling process requires ideas to be explored in real space and often long-standing assumptions are tested. If walls are built up from plans, do they make a building which is physically plausible or even possible? A good example of this was the series of fragmentary Anglo-Saxon archaeological features broadly interpreted as 'side chapels'.[7] These were extrapolated from the site plan, but it immediately became apparent that the arrangement was more complex than first thought. Once realistic roof pitches and junctions with the main walls were modelled, it became clear that there must have been a single-storey passage running along the outside of these internal chapels, possibly to allow practical access to either end of the church without intruding upon the liturgical space. This is not a feature extant in other churches, and was not evident from the archaeology alone, so is a new interpretation [Fig.63]. This experimental aspect of digital

---

[7] Cambridge, 2013, p.138.

Return outside

Fig.63: The cutaway of the interior showing the passage along the outside of the side-chapels

modelling as a research tool is an exciting, developing area and one which offers huge potential for better understanding some of the lost buildings of historic sites.

At the other end of the scale, the challenge of incorporating the very important but quite small sculptural fragments surviving from the Anglo-Saxon period, such as the animal frieze and grave-marker, was a difficult one. Hard for visitors to understand or engage with in abstraction, these fragments nevertheless offer a tangible window into this past environment. We were justifiably wary of implying that more was known than actually is, about their original location and arrangement.

We devised a presentation technique we called 'flying stones', which presents a digital version of the fragment, then digitally 'flies' it into a conjectural reconstruction. These are all rendered in simple grey scale to reinforce the speculative nature of the reconstructed setting. This proved very successful and the visual acknowledgement of uncertainty helped to allay academic fears about levels of accuracy and evidence. The later periods of development were dealt with on the same basis, a robust framework having emerged around making clear the evidential basis of our work. In each phase you can explore a cutaway view detailing the form and spatial arrangement of the church interior and find out more about the changes which shaped it. An overview and cutaway model of the crypt as originally laid out was also created, to give a sense of how that was used and experienced, as it is a space intentionally designed to disorientate. The touch-screen has a section entitled 'How did we do it?' which details the modelling and decision-making process [Fig.64]. In addition, each of the model phases is accompanied by explanatory text and supporting information.

As well as offering the opportunity to delve deeper, the layered text and use of grey scale does make clear what is known, what is reasonable conjecture and what is (currently) utterly unknown. It opens up to visitors the chance to think about evidence for themselves and connect the past with what they see today. In answer to the question of our title, "Would Wilfrid recognize this?", we hope he might think it looks vaguely familiar!

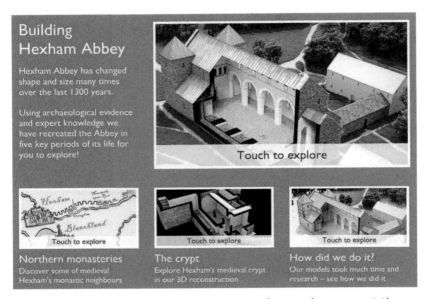

Fig.64: The interface as it appears on the touch-screen at the Abbey, showing the options visitors can explore

Envoi

"Hexham Abbey has ancient historic fabric on a scale not often seen in a parish church. ... The Abbey building is considered a wonder and plays a strong role in encouraging worshippers, visitors and tourists to the town."[1]

These are words from a recent study of Major Parish Churches. And the wonder is not only the building of the Abbey and its sizeable Priory Buildings, but the amount of interest, engagement, and considerable expertise that so many people bring to bear, as the pages of this book demonstrate. My thanks go to all contributors, especially to Richard Bailey, Chris Tolan-Smith, and Peter Richmond, and to the multitude of volunteers as well as to our staff team for all their support.

When I arrived here as Rector in 2015, I was aware of the huge changes that had occurred since my departure as Associate Vicar in 2006. Nonetheless, I probably had not taken on board fully how the Project had transformed the Abbey into the multi-faceted organization it now is. The effects of the project are still working their way through our self-understanding as a church community and as a staff and volunteer team.

The Project, generously funded with an HLF grant and the support of many donors, is presenting us with a great opportunity of focussing and reshaping our mission. One of the wonderful side-effects of the Project has been the kindling of learning and research, one of the fruits of which you can enjoy in this book. Education and learning about our heritage and about the Christian faith will continue to feature significantly in the life of the Abbey.

We are entrusted with a rich heritage and, as we move into the future, it is my hope and my prayer that the spirit of three foundational saints in the history of Hexham Abbey will live on in our generation as we are entrusted with this rich heritage: the generosity of Etheldreda who gave the land, the purposefulness and learning of Wilfrid who built the Abbey, and the prayerfulness and faith of Cuthbert.

The Revd Canon Dr Dagmar Winter
Rector and Lecturer of Hexham

---

[1] Historic England, 2016, p.59.

Bibliography

Anon. (1962) 'Vestments can teach us truths at Holy Communion', in *Hexham Abbey Chronicle* **46**, 4.

Anon (1984) *Hexham Abbey Chronicle* **310**, Oct 1984.

Alexander, J. (2013) 'The construction of the Gothic priory church of Hexham', in J. Ashbee and J. Luxford (eds), *Newcastle and Northumberland: Roman and Medieval Architecture and Art. (The British Archaeological Association Conference Transactions XXXVI)*. Leeds: Maney Publishing, 115–140.

Bailey, R. N. (2013) 'St. Wilfrid a European Anglo-Saxon', in N. J. Higham (ed.), *Wilfrid – Abbot, Bishop, Saint: Papers from the 1300th Anniversary Conferences*. Donington: Shaun Tyas, 112–123.

Bidwell, P. (2013) 'Wilfrid and Hexham: the Anglo-Saxon crypt', in N. J. Higham (ed.), *Wilfrid – Abbot, Bishop, Saint: Papers from the 1300th Anniversary Conferences*. Donington: Shaun Tyas, 153–162.

Brandwood, G. K. (1997) *Temple Moore: An Architect of the Late Gothic Revival*. Stamford: Paul Watkins Publishing.

Cambridge, E. (2013) 'The sources and function of Wilfrid's architecture at Ripon and Hexham', in N. J. Higham (ed.), *Wilfrid – Abbot, Bishop, Saint: Papers from the 1300th Anniversary Conferences*. Donington: Shaun Tyas, 136–151.

Cambridge, E. and Williams A. J. T. (1995) 'Hexham Abbey: a review of recent work and its implications', in *Archaeologia Aeliana* 5th series **23**, 51–138.

Carter, M. (2010) 'Remembrance, liturgy and status in a late medieval English Cistercian abbey: the mourning vestment of Abbot Robert Thornton of Jervaulx (1510–1533)', in *Textile History* **41:2**, 145–161.

Carter, M. (2013) 'Thornton, Robert (d. 1533)', in *Oxford Dictionary of National Biography*. Oxford University Press.

Ch'ng, E., Gaffney, V. and Chapman, H. (2013) *Visual Heritage in the Digital Age*. London: Springer.

CofE (2016) 'Section F: Things appertaining to churches' in *Canons of the Church of England*, 7th Edition. [www.churchofengland.org/about-us/structure/churchlawlegis/canons/canons-7th-edition.aspx].

Bibliography

Coldstream, N. (1995) 'The eastern chapels', in *Archaeologia Aeliana* 5th series **23**, 95–99.

Dugdale, W. (1655) *Monasticon Anglicanum...a History of the Abbies and Other Monasteries...and Cathedral and Collegiate Churches...in England and Wales.*

Fairless, J. (1853) *A Guide to the Abbey Church, &c., at Hexham, Northumberland.* Hexham: Edward Pruddah.

Freeland, J. (2006) *Aelred of Rievaulx: Lives of the Northern Saints.* Kalamazoo: Cistercian Publications.

Graham, F. (1984) *Hexham and Corbridge – A Short History and Guide.* Newcastle: author.

Hall, M. R. (1913) *English Church Needlework*, 2nd edition. London: Simpkin, Marshall, Hamilton, and Kent Co. Ltd.

Hart, S. (2012) *Medieval Church Window Tracery in England.* Martlesham: The Boydell Press.

Hefling, C. and Shattuck, C. (eds) (2006) *The Oxford Guide to the Book of Common Prayer — a Worldwide Survey.* Oxford: University Press.

Historic England (2016) 'Hexham, the Priory and Parish Church of St Andrew (Hexham Abbey)' in *Sustaining Major Parish Churches – Appendix J: 12 In-Depth Case Studies, October 2016*, 58–75.

Hodges, C. C. (1888) *Ecclesia Hagustaldensis. The Abbey of St Andrew Hexham.* Privately printed for the author.

Hodges, C. C. (1913) *Guide to the Priory Church of Saint Andrew, Hexham.* Hexham: Gibson and Son.

Hodges, C. C. and Gibson, J. (1919) *Hexham and its Abbey.* Hexham: Gibson and Son.

Hodges, C. C. (1924) 'The conventual buildings of the Priory of Hexham, with a description of a recently discovered twin capital from the cloisters', in *Archaeologia Aeliana* 3rd series **21**, 214–223.

Hutchinson, W. (1776–8) *A View of Northumberland, with an Excursion to the Abbey of Mailross in Scotland.* Newcastle.

Jennings, D. (2001) 'Restoration of the Abbey: Savage versus Lockhart', in *Hexham Historian* **11**, 48–70.

Kendrick, A. (1902) Victoria and Albert Museum: Keeper's Report, 21/06/1902, RP. 87187/1902.

Marshall, F. and Marshall, H. (1894) *Old English Embroidery: its techniques and symbolism*. London: Horace Cox.

Messent, J. (1993) *Design Sources for Symbolism*. Trowbridge: Redwood Books.

Ryder, P. F. (2014) 'The arms of Sir Reynold Carnaby at Hexham Abbey House, 1539', in *The Coat of Arms* 3rd series **10**, 27–31.

Savage, E. S. and Hodges, C. C. (1907) *A record of all works connected with Hexham Abbey since January 1899 and now in progress: also an account of St. Wilfrid's Cathedral, various antiquities, Mr. Temple Moore's Report upon the proposed works, an estimate of their cost, and an appeal to the public for subscriptions*. Hexham: J. Catherall & Co.

Smelt, H. (1985) 'Church vestments', in *Abbey Chronicle* **316**, 2; **317**, 3; and **318**, 3.

Taylor, R. (2004) *How to Read a Church*. London: Rider.

Taylor, W. T. (1965) *Hexham Abbey 674–1965* 6th edition. Hexham: R. Robson & Sons, The Abbey Press.

Todd, N. (1975) 'Trade unions and the engineering industry dispute at Barrow-in-Furness 1897–98', in *International Review of Social History* **20:1**, 33–47.

Webb, J. (2004) *The Age of Bede — Bede: Life of Cuthbert | Eddius Stephanus: Life of Wilfrid | Bede: Lives of the Abbots of Wearmouth and Jarrow | The Anonymous History of Abbot Ceolfrith | with the Voyage of St Brendan*. 2nd edition London: Penguin.

Whittick, A. (1935) *Symbol for Designers: a Handbook on the Application of Symbols and Symbolism to Design*. London: Crosby Lockwood & Son.

Wiechec, P. (1980) *Celtic Quilt Designs*. Sunnyvale USA: Celtic Design Co.

Wood, J. (1826) *Plan of Hexham from actual survey. Published as the Act directs*. Sold at Hexham and by J.Wood, Barnard Castle. Printed by Robertson and Ballantine, 18, Greenside Place, Edinburgh.

Index

Bold page numbers indicate figures.

Lightning Source UK Ltd.
Milton Keynes UK
UKOW07f1115250617
304040UK00011B/53/P

9 780952 761594